FROM THE FILMS OF

Harry Potter ™

THE BROOM COLLECTION

FROM THE FILMS OF

Harry Potter

™

THE BROOM COLLECTION
& OTHER ARTEFACTS FROM THE WIZARDING WORLD

JODY REVENSON

BLOOMSBURY
CHILDREN'S BOOKS
LONDON   OXFORD   NEW YORK   NEW DELHI   SYDNEY

CONTENTS

INTRODUCTION

In the Muggle world, brooms are simple, commonplace objects. Unassuming things, they are used for sweeping floors or brushing debris out of the door. In the wizarding world, however, brooms are so much more.

In the Harry Potter films, wizarding broomsticks are magical artefacts that enable their riders to soar from one place to another. They can be used to dodge dangerous dragons, escape Death Eaters and other Dark forces, or simply to take to the skies. They are also used in thrilling competitions. Brooms are an integral part of the wizarding world's favourite sport: the action-packed game of Quidditch, played by two teams who rocket through the air. In this high-flying game, having a fast, new racing broom is an advantage indeed, and the pages of *The Daily Prophet* contain many advertisements showcasing the latest models of the day.

Broom designs are as varied as their uses, and many brooms even have personal touches. *Harry Potter: The Broom Collection* takes a closer look at the magic brooms of the Harry Potter films, their makers and their riders. From the film-makers who designed and crafted them to the actors and characters who rode them – all played a part in making these enchanted brooms come to life on-screen.

BROOMS IN THE WIZARDING WORLD

BROOMS ARE AN ESSENTIAL COMPONENT of Harry Potter's adventures as he navigates his years at Hogwarts School of Witchcraft and Wizardry. For Harry, his broomstick is almost as important as his wand. In *Harry Potter and the Philosopher's Stone*, it is Harry's natural broom-flying ability that keeps his friends safe from a flock of flying keys, which is one challenge to solve as they pursue the Stone.

In *Harry Potter and the Goblet of Fire*, for the Triwizard Tournament's first task – getting past an angry dragon that protects the second task's clue – Harry summons his broom for his advantage. He outflies the Hungarian Horntail and grabs the clue for a victory.

However, it is at Quidditch that Harry excels, becoming the youngest player in a century on the Gryffindor team. When he is chosen to join, he is gifted a Nimbus 2000, the fastest broom on the market, and later, a Firebolt. It doesn't matter what broom he uses, though. Harry's skill at flying is extraordinary.

Brooms are often as personal to the owners as are their wands, and the concept artists and prop makers behind the Harry Potter films sought to reflect each flyer's personality in their designs. The broom flown by the flamboyant Nymphadora Tonks has colourful branches placed throughout the bristle head. The broom of Arthur Weasley, a great lover of Muggle-made objects, has the pedals and basket of a non-magic bicycle. And the broom of Alastor 'Mad-Eye' Moody, a renegade Auror, calls to mind a showy chopper motorbike.

EARLY BROOM DESIGNS

"Welcome to your first flying lesson."

Madam Hooch, *Harry Potter and the Philosopher's Stone*

Should a broom be practical and understated, or wild and colourful? Should it be streamlined for speed or equipped with ribbons and personal touches? Some of the earliest ideas for the brooms to be seen (and flown) in the Harry Potter films were drawn by concept artist Gert Stevens. The concept and visual development artists would reference the Harry Potter novels by author J.K. Rowling and confer with production designer Stuart Craig, who developed the overall visual look for the films.

Stevens' first designs helped establish a basic approach to the shapes of the brooms' handles, but with a decidedly whimsical attitude. Among these initial broom designs, one uses very unconventional purple opaque plastic 'twigs' for the bristle head, a saddle-style seat and a kickstand perhaps used for mounting. A second broom has a typical bristle head of branches bound by a collar and wrapped in a purple tie. However, this broom also has another head at the top of its curved handle – that of a stylised sculpted dragon.

THE BROOM MAKERS

In the wizarding world, making brooms is a competitive business. While the Nimbus Racing Broom Company might have found success with the Nimbus 2000 and Nimbus 2001 models, each considered the fastest broom on offer at its time, the Firebolt takes over as the fastest broom in *Harry Potter and the Prisoner of Azkaban*.

For the Harry Potter films, the process of constructing a broom began with artwork. Visual development artists would create designs for brooms that often reflected the personality of their riders. Dozens of sketches might be submitted to production designer Stuart Craig before final approval and construction. "You keep going until they're happy with it," says Adam Brockbank, who contributed ideas for the brooms of Order of the Phoenix members, among others. "It's important to find a core idea about the broomstick and how it relates to the character." Brockbank's only frustration was that intricate detailing on the broomsticks was often covered by the riders' robes. "You never really get a good look at them," he says. "They're flown very quickly!"

Once a design was approved, art director Hattie Storey's team of artists drafted broom blueprints, outlining the length, material, curvature, as well as any other finishes or detailing – such as showing distinctive nodules or how the runes along the Firebolt should be applied to the broomstick.

With blueprints in hand, the task of constructing the brooms for the Quidditch games played at Hogwarts fell to the props department. Fitting for racing brooms, the prop makers' most important consideration was to make the brooms both strong and lightweight. "These weren't just props that the kids carried around," explains prop department head, Pierre Bohanna. "They had to sit on them. They had to be mounted on to motion-control bases for special effects shots, and twisted and turned to imitate flying, so they had to be very thin and incredibly durable." To that effect, aircraft-grade titanium was used for the brooms' cores. Next, the shafts and handles were covered with mahogany wood. The bristle heads were made from birch branches.

Not all brooms seen in the Harry Potter films are flown, however. For *Harry Potter and the Goblet of Fire*, assistant buyer Tamazin Simmonds required a large quantity of brooms that did not need to fly, so she made contact with a broom-making family in Tadley, Hampshire, who happened to be the official besom (twig) 'broom squires' for Buckingham Palace. More than eighty brooms were constructed for the film out of large birch and hazel branches. The material for these brooms was collected in the winter, when there is no sap in the wood. The branches must dry for six months before the bark can be shaved down to the requested circumference of the handle, or 'tail'.

The bristle head of these brooms was made from twigs taken from the crown of the tree. First, longer, rougher twigs are rolled together, then they are surrounded by shorter, smoother twigs, and the bundle is tied with wire for the strongest bind. Finally, the tails are inserted into the heads and secured with a nail or wooden peg. Every part of this process, which this broom-making family has been undertaking for 300 years, was done by hand, with no machinery involved.

BROOM SELLERS IN DIAGON ALLEY

Diagon Alley is the wizarding world's marketplace in London, with shops featuring magical creatures, cascades of cauldrons and of course, brooms. Harry Potter takes his first trip there in *Harry Potter and the Philosopher's Stone* to buy his first-year school supplies. As he walks down the street, Harry notices several children his age crowded around Quality Quidditch Supplies – a shop devoted to fans of the wizarding sport. Harry doesn't even know what Quidditch is at the time, but he is enthralled by the object of the crowd's fascination – the new Nimbus 2000 broomstick, the fastest model yet for flying, which is hovering in a display window.

Quality Quidditch Supplies carries all the equipment needed for the sport as well as fan-related sportswear branded with the colours and logos of Britain and Ireland's professional Quidditch teams. The set designers created displays with mannequins wearing robes for the Chudley Cannons and Holyhead Harpies. Banners for other teams, including Puddlemere United, Ballycastle Bats and Montrose Magpies are strung in the shop windows' backgrounds. At the back of the shop is a rack of brooms that patrons are invited to test-fly, but 'All Breakages Must Be Paid For'.

In addition to Quality Quidditch Supplies, there is a second shop on Diagon Alley that sells brooms, although their stock consists of used models, or as the shop's sign declares, 'nearly new brooms'. The aptly named 2nd Hand Brooms shop has stacks of bedraggled brooms displayed outside its walls.

Set decorator Stephenie McMillan was tasked with finding large numbers of brooms to use on the Diagon Alley set in *Harry Potter and the Philosopher's Stone* – though her team was forbidden from revealing what the purchases were for as they gathered the brooms from bargain shops and outdoor marketplaces. To get around this embargo, one resourceful crew member explained to a shopkeeper that the reason she needed so many broomsticks was because she had a lot of sweeping to do!

FLYING CLASS TRAINING BROOMS

"Up!"

First-year students, *Harry Potter and the Philosopher's Stone*

First-year students at Hogwarts are required to take a Flying Class to learn broom-flying techniques. The instructor is Madam Rolanda Hooch, who also referees the Hogwarts Quidditch team matches and has eyes like a hawk's – literally. Brooms are supplied to the students by the school, but their scraggly, knobby look speaks to years, perhaps centuries, of use.

The first lesson is simply to raise your broom into your grasp. Directing the students to stand on the left side of their broomstick, Madam Hooch tells them to hold their right hand over the broom and give the command "Up!". Almost immediately, Harry Potter's broom flies into his hand. To Hermione Granger's frustration, her broom refuses to rise, and when Ron Weasley's broom soars up, it accidentally hits him in the face.

The brooms used by the young actors in the flying lesson in *Harry Potter and the Philosopher's Stone* were seemingly simple constructions of a birch handle nailed to a bristle head wrapped together with willow wood, as they would not actually be flying them, with the exception of Harry Potter, Draco Malfoy and Neville Longbottom. Care was taken to keep an organic look to the brooms, giving them knobby ridges and raised nodules for a natural appearance.

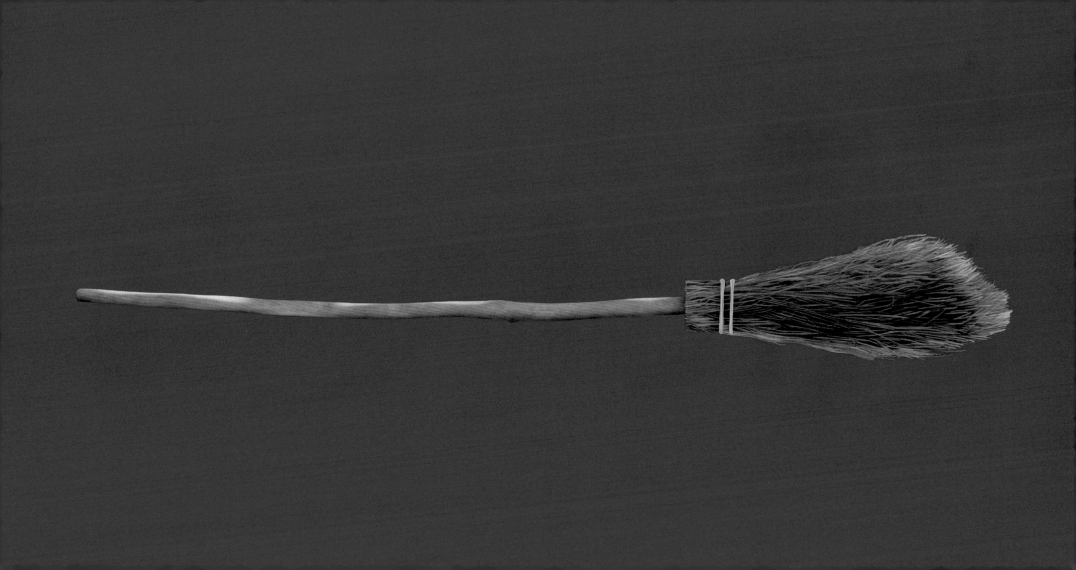

THE FIRST TO FLY

As the initial flying lesson continues, Madam Hooch tells the students to mount their brooms, push up off the ground and hover steadily for a moment before touching back down. Immediately upon her whistle mark, Neville Longbottom floats up into the air but cannot lower himself, suddenly taking off for a wild flight around the Hogwarts quadrangle.

"I had read about this in the script but had no idea what to expect," says actor Matthew Lewis, who plays Neville. For the start of his flight, Lewis's broom was attached to a blue-screen-covered pole, which itself was suspended from a crane. On cue, the crane would raise Lewis into the air. "It was very weird to come to work," he recalls, "and to be put on a broomstick and hang in the air, but it was also very cool." Lewis admits that he wasn't keen on heights at the time, but the opportunity to do the stunt made him want to tackle his fear even more.

The remainder of Neville's flight was filmed on a blue-screened studio set covered in crash mats. For the actors' comfort while riding the simple besom brooms, a bicycle seat was attached between the bristle head and handle, then concealed by their cloaks.

FLYING AMONG THE WINGED KEYS

Brooms are not the only items that fly in the wizarding world. In *Harry Potter and the Philosopher's Stone*, Harry, Ron and Hermione face a series of challenges as they search for the Philosopher's Stone to prevent it from being stolen from Hogwarts. In one of these tests, they enter a room chock-full of winged, flying keys and a single hovering broom, which resembles one of the flying class practice brooms. When the charm *Alohomora* doesn't unlock the door that leads to the next challenge, the three heroes realise they must find the right winged key. Harry mounts the broom and succeeds in catching the correct key as he chases the flock around the room.

Physical keys and sample wings were created, "but were only used as reference or a guide for the visual effects department to generate the thousands of flying keys that were in that chamber," says Pierre Bohanna. The only key that was physically used in the scene was the one that Harry catches, which appears old and rusty. "The idea was that there were lots of glamorous keys, but only one dull, flat key," he adds. Digital artists modelled the movements of the keys to resemble the flight patterns of a flock of birds.

BROOM ADVERTISEMENTS

Graphic artists Miraphora Mina and Eduardo Lima were tasked with providing ancillary material for the pages of the wizarding newspaper, *The Daily Prophet*, which were filled with crossword puzzles, sports updates and a myriad of advertisements. The team mined J.K. Rowling's novels for ideas, and once approved by the author, added their own extrapolated suggestions, which contributed to the culture of wizarding society. For example, they created an ad for the Nimbus Company's station-wagon-type broom, the 'Fambus', which can seat an entire family, as well as ads for help when your broom has lost its vroom, which were interspersed throughout the *Daily Prophet*'s pages.

THE SPORT OF QUIDDITCH

THE MOST POPULAR WIZARD SPORT is Quidditch, which is played while flying on broomsticks. Each team has seven players: three Chasers, two Beaters, a Keeper and a Seeker. Chasers try to score points by throwing a ball called a Quaffle through one of three hoop-shaped goalposts on the opposite team's side. The Keeper for the team guards these hoops and tries to prevent the Quaffle from scoring a goal, worth ten points. At the same time, two bewitched balls called Bludgers fly around the Quidditch pitch trying to knock players off of their brooms. Beaters use bats to hit the Bludgers away from their own teammates or aim them at the opposing team. Finally, the Seeker's job is to catch the Golden Snitch, worth 150 points, which ends the game.

"It was important that Quidditch felt dangerous, that it felt fast, and that – for lack of a better word – it felt cool," says *Harry Potter and the Philosopher's Stone* director Chris Columbus. "You wanted every kid who saw the movie to say, 'That would be my favourite sport, if I could play any sport.'" Production designer Stuart Craig circled the Quidditch pitch with tall square towers. "[These] were the way to have the fans in a position where they could actually see the action," Craig explains. The towers also allowed players to fly around them in order to create a sense of speed.

In this section, we'll profile the racing brooms seen in the Harry Potter films, as well as the Golden Snitch and other pieces of Quidditch equipment.

HARRY POTTER'S NIMBUS 2000

"That's not just a broomstick, Harry. It's a Nimbus 2000!"

Ron Weasley, *Harry Potter and the Philosopher's Stone*

When Neville is injured during broom practice in *Harry Potter and the Philosopher's Stone*, he's taken to the infirmary by Madam Hooch, and Slytherin Draco Malfoy picks up the Remembrall that has fallen from Neville's pocket. Draco ascends on his broom and it is here Harry Potter's natural talent for flying is quickly evident. Harry flies up and demands Draco hand the Remembrall over to him, then streaks through the air to retrieve it when Draco flings it away. Harry catches it just before making a breathtaking sudden stop in front of the tower office window of head of Gryffindor house, Professor McGonagall. Impressed by his ability, she recommends him to be the new Seeker for the Gryffindor Quidditch team, and right before his first game, she gifts Harry with the newest, fastest flying broom model of the day – the Nimbus 2000.

The Nimbus 2000 is a refined besom broom with a brown lacquered handle and streamlined bristle head bound in three thin gold-plated bands. The broom's logo is engraved in gold at the tip of its handle. In addition to the bicycle seat that was bolted to the broom for flying sequences, a set of foot pedals was added that would cradle the actors' legs as they 'flew'. "[The film-makers] wanted the actors to ride the brooms like jockeys with their feet tucked underneath," says Pierre Bohanna. Unlike the seats, the foot pedals were a visible part of each broom's design.

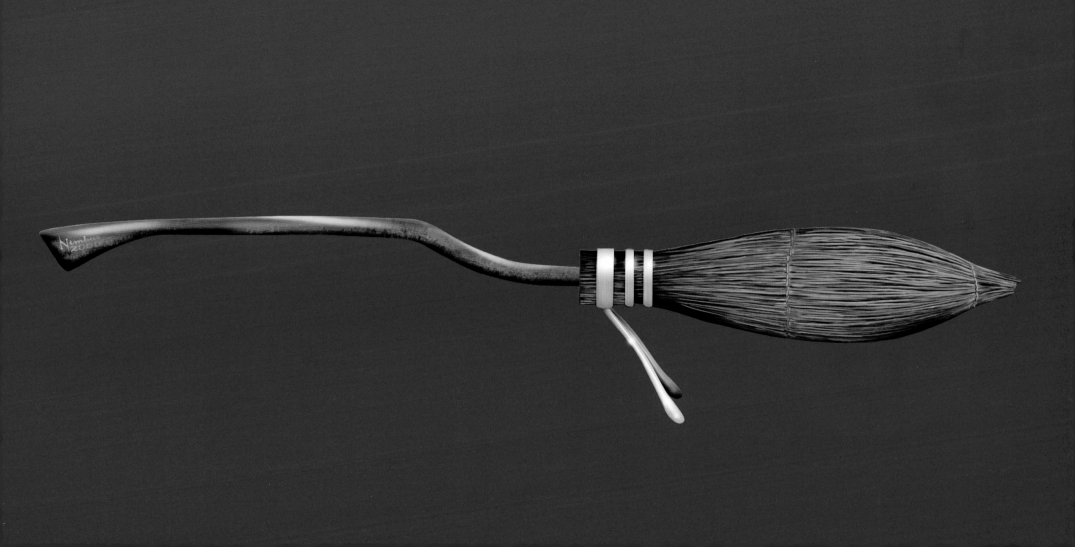

DRACO MALFOY'S NIMBUS 2001

"You see Weasley, unlike some, my father can afford the best."

Draco Malfoy, *Harry Potter and the Chamber of Secrets*

In *Harry Potter and the Chamber of Secrets*, the Gryffindor Quidditch team practice is pre-empted by the Slytherin team needing to work with its new Seeker – Draco Malfoy. Draco is flying on the newest Nimbus model, the Nimbus 2001. In fact, the entire Slytherin team has Nimbus 2001s, bought for them by Draco's father, Lucius.

The jet-black Nimbus 2001 has a straight handle that ends in an almost snakehead-shaped tip, engraved in silver with the 2001 logo. The neatly clipped bristle head is bound in a wide silver band. Unique to this broom, its foot pedals are, literally, pedals similar to a bicycle's, but the broom rider still hooks their ankles over them as do riders on other types of brooms.

In the studio, the broomsticks were mounted on a hydraulic pole with a seat at the end for the actors. "The attachment was adjustable," says special effects supervisor John Richardson, "so the pole could swing in any direction. We then adapted that so the pole could be rigged from above or below the actor, for scenes where the kids are upside down or hanging from their brooms." To ensure their safety, the actors were strapped to the seats with climbing harnesses attached across the groin and at the back.

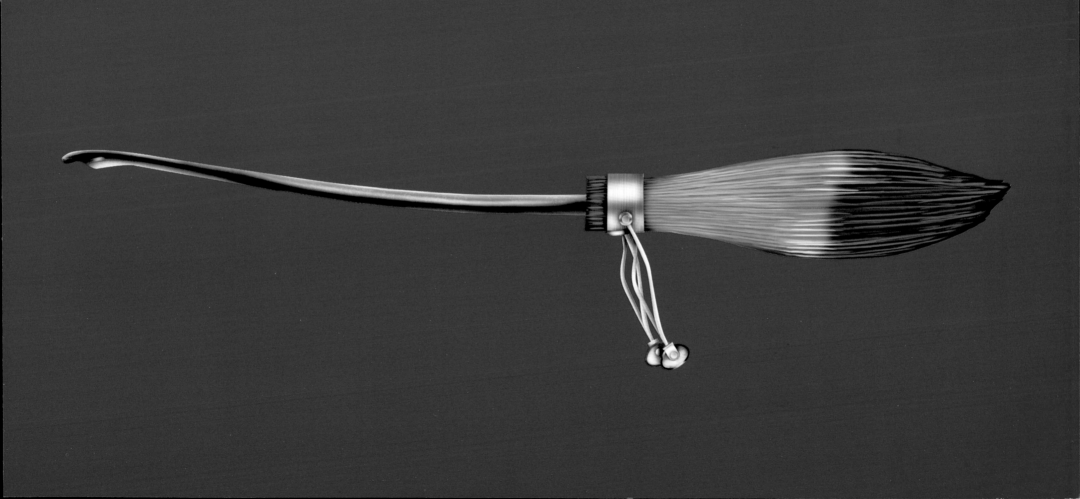

HARRY POTTER'S FIREBOLT

"I didn't mean to open it Harry. It was badly wrapped. They made me do it!"

Ron Weasley, *Harry Potter and the Prisoner of Azkaban*

During a Quidditch game held in a fierce thunderstorm in *Harry Potter and the Prisoner of Azkaban*, Dementors circle the Quidditch pitch, causing Harry to lose control of his broom and fall from the sky when confronted by the Dark creatures. Harry is saved when Headmaster Albus Dumbledore uses the *Arresto Momentum* Charm, but sadly his Nimbus 2000 is blown into the Whomping Willow and thoroughly destroyed. At the end of the events in *Prisoner of Azkaban*, Harry is gifted a Firebolt broom by his newly discovered godfather, Sirius Black. The Firebolt surpasses the Nimbus line in speed, and Harry doesn't wait to try it out.

Prior to the filming of *Prisoner of Azkaban*, director Alfonso Cuarón commissioned new wands for the actors with more organic designs and exotic woods. The Firebolt also reflects this new aesthetic. The handle is made from a knobby dark wood that twists out of the bristle head. It straightens through to the tip, but only the top of the handle is shaved smooth and polished. There is a line of ten symbols etched in gold along this section, which visual development artist Dermot Power suggested would have been burned into the wood. The bristle head itself is trimmed, though not as smoothly as for the Nimbuses, and bound with two silver bands.

EMBELLISHING THE FIREBOLT

Visual development artist Dermot Power created studies for the Firebolt's unique finish based on a heavily burred handle with a planed top and a natural, rough underside. Golden rune symbols were branded on to the planed wood surface and continued all the way down the handle. The rune choices were provided by the art department.

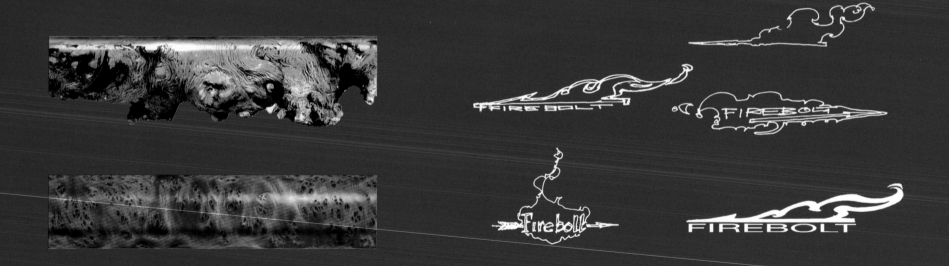

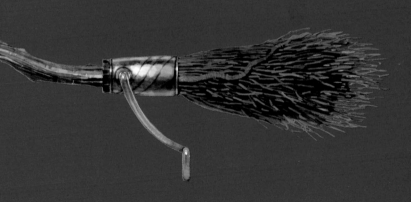

RON WEASLEY'S BROOM

"Weasley! Weasley! Weasley!"

Gryffindor fans, *Harry Potter and the Half-Blood Prince*

There were no Quidditch games filmed for *Harry Potter and the Goblet of Fire* (the Triwizard Tournament pre-empted them) or *Harry Potter and the Order of the Phoenix* (Hogwarts' temporary Headmistress Dolores Umbridge cancelled them), so when actor Rupert Grint (Ron Weasley) read that Quidditch was a major part of the story of *Harry Potter and the Half-Blood Prince*, he was thrilled. "I knew the audience was really looking forward to seeing Quidditch again, because we hadn't had it for a while," says Grint. "But I was really excited, particularly for Ron," he adds, "and I finally got to sit on a broom and fly for the first time."

Ron's broom is modest, perhaps as a nod to his family's financial situation. It features a light wood handle, silver pedals and a long bristle tail that has a bit of an upturn at the end. Prior to *Half-Blood Prince*, the only time Ron was seen with a broom, it hit him in the face during his first Flying Class.

After winning the role of Keeper on the Gryffindor Quidditch team (thanks to some help from Hermione), Ron's anxiety mounts before his first Quidditch match. Thankfully, Harry figures out a way for his friend to believe in himself, pretending to slip the good luck potion Felix Felicis in his drink, giving Ron overwhelming confidence. "He makes a few saves, so he gets a bit cocky," says Grint, "and that was really fun to play, because that's a side to Ron I didn't usually get to do in the films."

CORMAC MCLAGGEN'S BROOM

"No hard feelings, eh, Weasley? ... I'll be trying out for Gryffindor Keeper, too. Nothing personal."

Cormac McLaggen, *Harry Potter and the Half-Blood Prince*

Ron Weasley's competition for the role of Keeper is the incredibly agile (and slightly arrogant) Cormac McLaggen, played by Freddie Stroma. McLaggen is not only interested in becoming Keeper, he tells Ron, but also in the opportunity to get to know Hermione Granger "on a first-name basis."

In order to express a difference in the physical size of the two wannabe Keepers, McLaggen tries out with a broom that is a bit taller and wider than the other players' equipment, in order to accommodate what Ron suggests is Cormac's "Beater's build". The broom is in the same style as Viktor Krum's, with both the wood of the handle and the foot pedals rendered in a dull brass-coloured finish. The tail's twigs are roughly arranged.

Cormac proves a worthy adversary for Ron, whose nerves are getting the best of him. Hermione Granger decides to sneakily help her friend out with a Confundus Charm, causing Cormac to miss too many Quaffles and lose out on the position.

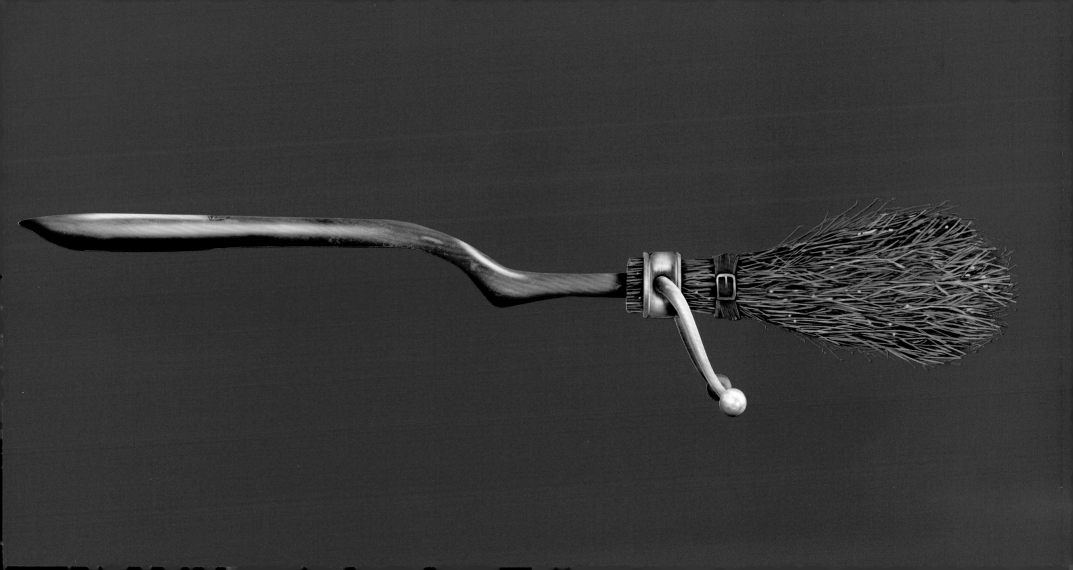

FRED AND GEORGE WEASLEY'S BROOMS

"Our job is to make sure you don't get bloodied up too bad."

"Can't make any promises, of course. Rough game, Quidditch!"

Fred and George Weasley, *Harry Potter and the Philosopher's Stone*

Fred and George Weasley are the Beaters on the Gryffindor Quidditch team when Harry Potter joins as Seeker; they hit the lively Bludgers with short wooden bats. The brooms the twins ride in *Harry Potter and the Philosopher's Stone* are unassuming; they feature the simplest besom construction of handle and bristle head.

While filming the Quidditch scenes during the production of *Philosopher's Stone*, the actors were asked to not give away the secrets of how it was done, so "when people asked how we filmed the scenes, we used to let on that it was all done with parachutes," says Oliver Phelps (George). "Or that we went skydiving, that's how they shot it," adds his twin, James (Fred). Another account they gave was that they would hang on a rope outside the back of an aeroplane.

During the events of *Harry Potter and the Order of the Phoenix*, the entrepreneurial twins decide to leave Hogwarts and depart amid a fantastic display of fireworks, shooting them off around the Great Hall while flying on flashy new broomsticks more suited to their characters. The branches of the horn-shaped bristle heads on the twins' brooms are decidedly orange. Fred has painted the scarlet-and-gold Gryffindor house colours in circles near the top of his handle and tied leather straps around it. George's broom has the name 'WEASLEY' carved on to the handle, with a star

GINNY WEASLEY'S BROOM

"Shut it!"

Ginny Weasley, *Harry Potter and the Half-Blood Prince*

When Harry Potter holds tryouts for the sixth-year team in *Harry Potter and the Half-Blood Prince*, he's ably assisted by Ginny Weasley, the youngest of the seven Weasley siblings and a very competent Quidditch player. "I think you see a lot of Ginny's confidence come through," says actress Bonnie Wright, who plays Ginny, "as well as an undercurrent of her competitive, even overconfident, self."

Ginny is a Chaser on the team and flies a broom with a straight handle similar to Ron's. The bristle head of her broom, which is held together by a belt, flares out instead of up, unlike Ron's, and the branches become redder towards the end. Ginny's skills are quite impressive – as Chaser, she is either catching, holding or throwing a Quaffle, so she frequently flies her broom with only one hand on the handle.

Bonnie Wright had heard stories from other cast members about broomstick flying over the years. "Some had said, 'Oh, it's the most horrible thing,' and others said it was really fun," she recalls. For her, at first, it was scary. "I'm not afraid of heights, but they manage to get you quite high on these complex hydraulic broomstick systems. It's not all done by computer," she continues. "You actually do a lot of the action yourself. I did one [manoeuvre] where I was spinning completely horizontally, three hundred and sixty degrees, and I was like, 'Whoa!'"

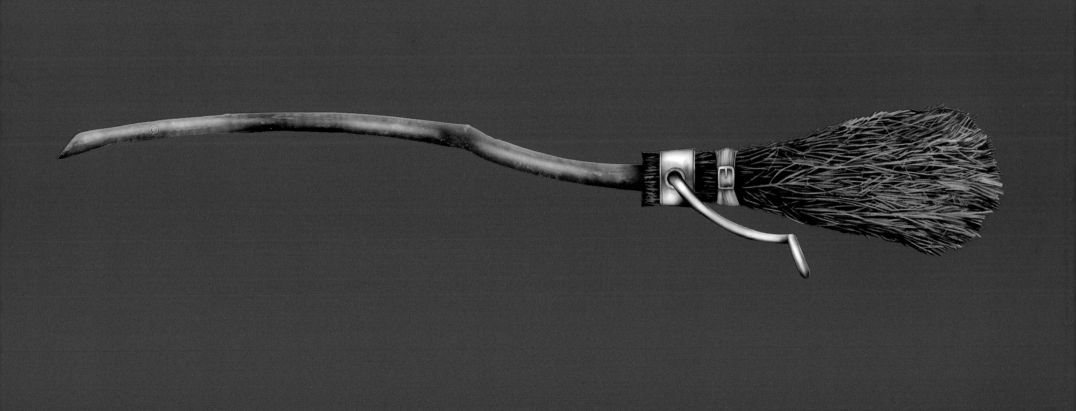

QUIDDITCH EQUIPMENT CRATE

Once Harry Potter becomes Seeker for the Gryffindor Quidditch team in *Harry Potter and the Philosopher's Stone*, team captain Oliver Wood gives him a one-on-one lesson on the game. In preparation, Harry helps Wood carry out a well-worn crate that contains the balls used in the sport: the large Quaffle in the centre, two Bludgers strapped down with chains and the Golden Snitch.

Early designs for the crate included elaborate clamps, buckles and metal corner bumpers. The version that made it to the screen, however, followed prop maker Pierre Bohanna's philosophy that the school's equipment would typically be rough and worn from use. The graphics department created the eight colourfully designed coats of arms on display on the inside lid of the crate, placing them around a small hinged shield featuring the animals from the four Hogwarts houses. Behind the centre shield is the Golden Snitch, removable once the doors of the shield are popped open.

The final design of the Quidditch equipment crate was a collaboration between the prop department, graphics department and special effects team, who made the crate rock and rattle from the clattering, impatient movements of the two Bludgers.

QUAFFLE

"There are three kinds of balls. This one's called the Quaffle."

Oliver Wood, *Harry Potter and the Philosopher's Stone*

The Quaffle is the largest ball used in Quidditch, similar in appearance to a Muggle basketball or football. Even though the game ends with one team's capture of the Golden Snitch, mathematically, if enough Quaffle throws are scored, the opposing team could still end up winning the match.

The Quaffle was first built in what is called a 'patent,' which is a wax version of the ball. "It's a master shape that we make our moulds from," says Pierre Bohanna. The mould yielded a foam core that was wrapped in red sheet wax to give it a leather-like texture. The ball was debossed with a faded Hogwarts crest and beaten-up stitching suggestive of years of use. "That was the general feel of all the Quidditch equipment," Bohanna says. "It was well used; it was school equipment. Everything was pretty worn and knackered." In total, four Quaffles were made for *Harry Potter and the Philosopher's Stone*.

Each ball created for Quidditch was assigned an individual sound as it flew through the air. The Quaffle makes a decided 'thunk' when it is caught by a player.

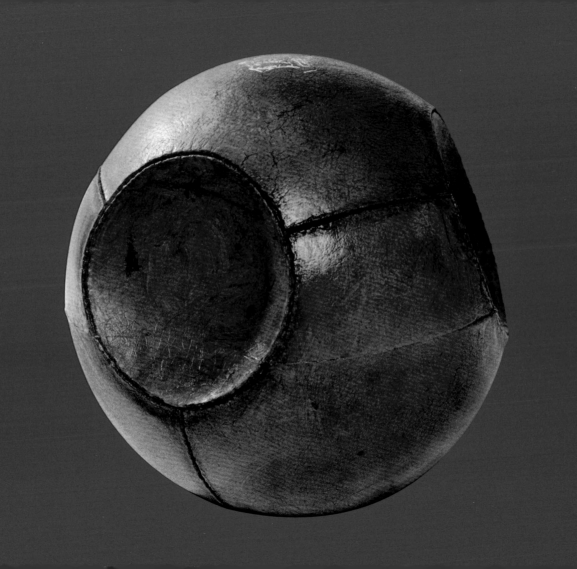

BLUDGER

"Careful now, it's coming back."

Oliver Wood, *Harry Potter and the Philosopher's Stone*

Bludgers are the heaviest balls used in Quidditch and dangerous even in the most innocuous games. In *Harry Potter and the Chamber of Secrets*, an enchanted 'rogue' Bludger goes after Harry during a match with Slytherin. During its pursuit, the Bludger breaks the broomstick of captain Oliver Wood, then continues to attack Harry, pursuing him around the pitch and eventually crashing into Harry's right arm as he reaches for the Snitch. Even when Harry lands on the ground with the Snitch in his left hand, the Bludger continues to attack until Hermione blows it up with the *Finite Incantatem* counterspell.

In the wizarding world, Bludgers are made out of iron. The prop makers took this into consideration for their first approach, constructing the Bludger out of a combination of steel and wood. This version was a bit too heavy to work with, so the final iteration was made from resin and rubber. In order to have the Bludgers look metallic, iron powder was applied to the exterior, then an acid was used to give them an aged, rusty appearance.

Oliver Wood describes the Bludgers as "nasty little buggers", and so the sound designers agreed that when they fly off after being struck, they should sound like angry animals. Sound designer Martin Cantwell recorded his own voice for the Bludgers, channelling the Tasmanian devil to give them its outraged, chittering sound.

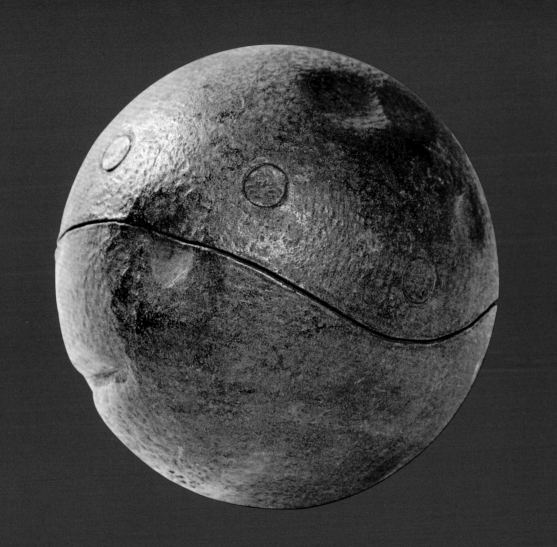

THE GOLDEN SNITCH

"You catch this Potter, and we win."

Oliver Wood, *Harry Potter and the Philosopher's Stone*

Opening up the box of Quidditch equipment, Oliver Wood shows Harry the Quaffle, the Bludgers and finally the Golden Snitch, possibly the most important ball in the sport. Taking the golden sphere into his hand, Harry declares that he likes that ball. "Ah, you like it now," Wood responds. "Just wait. It's wicked fast and damn near impossible to see."

The walnut-sized Snitch would zip and zoom around the Quidditch pitch digitally, but it did need to be believably aerodynamic in its design, which featured fluttering silver wings. Production designer Stuart Craig and visual development artist Gert Stevens developed Snitches with fish fins, helicopter seeds and dragonfly wings before deciding on the shape of a ship's sail made from carved slats. An additional caveat was that "[the wings] must be completely hidden while at rest," says Craig. Given this instruction, Pierre Bohanna and his prop making team sculpted an art nouveau-style design for the Snitch. "The wings are stowed in deep narrow channels curving across the surface," says Craig, "apparently surface decoration, but secretly hiding the wings."

The physical Snitch was electroformed in copper and gold-plated. Sound designers assigned it the murmur of hummingbird wings and digital artists added a reflection of the Snitch in Harry's glasses whenever it flew past "the youngest Seeker in a century".

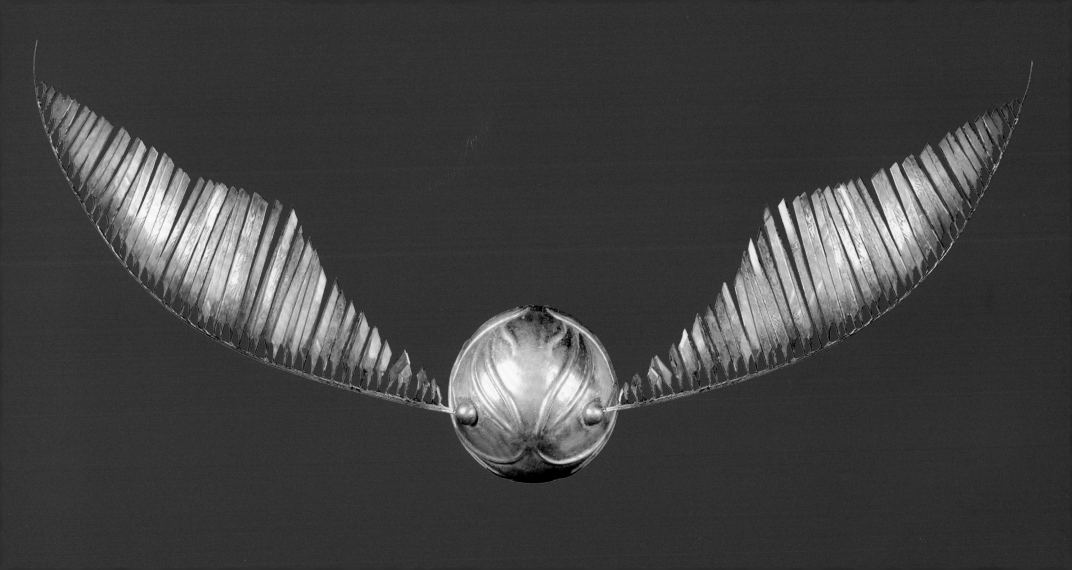

BEATER BATS AND BAYS

"You better take this."

Oliver Wood, *Harry Potter and the Philosopher's Stone*

Though Beater bats must be strong enough to knock away a ball known to be made of iron in the game of Quidditch, in *filming* Quidditch, the bats used by the actors needed to be light and manoeuvrable. "[The bats] were originally made out of wood and were way too heavy," says Pierre Bohanna. The final Beater bats were made from fibreglass and rubber, and then worked to look as if they were made from wood with steel reinforcements and a comfortable wrapped grip.

As any player could be the target of a Bludger ball, padding was an essential part of the Quidditch uniform. Special arm guards based on cricket players' safety equipment were designed for the team uniforms. Called 'Bays', they were buckled around the arms and overlapped the players' leather gloves. Other padding pieces for arms and legs recalled the protective leather coverings of 1930s American football.

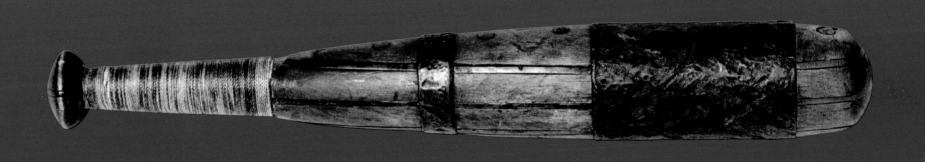

HOGWARTS QUIDDITCH SCHOOL TROPHIES

In *Harry Potter and the Goblet of Fire*, Hogwarts hosts the Triwizard Tournament, a competition between the three European wizarding schools that encourages international magical cooperation. After the champions are announced, they assemble in the Trophy Room for photos and interviews for *The Daily Prophet*.

The school's Trophy Room is jam-packed with hundreds of plaques, medals, awards and trophies huge and small, especially for winners of the annual Quidditch Cup. There are also individual Quidditch trophies for Seekers, Beaters and Chasers. The prop department scoured local antique markets and auctions for real trophies or found objects that could be redesigned into wizard trophies and added their own original creations to the pile.

The trophies were inscribed with names taken from the novels by J.K. Rowling, along with names of fellow crew or family members. Individual Quidditch award winners included Charlie Weasley, Ron's brother, who won when he was a Seeker on the Gryffindor team, and Oliver Wood, who received the Award for Effort.

RAVENCLAW
1962

QUIDDITCH UNIFORMS AND FAN WEAR

HOGWARTS QUIDDITCH UNIFORMS – YEARS ONE AND TWO

Quidditch is a rough and fast-moving sport, and the uniforms worn by players in *Harry Potter and the Philosopher's Stone* needed to offer protection, but also enough flexibility for the players to manoeuvre. There's also the question of age – Quidditch dates back roughly a thousand years, so how contemporary should the uniforms really be? Ultimately, "we wanted this to look cool to kids, but not modern," says costume designer Judianna Makovsky. The students' academic wear had been based on nineteenth-century English boarding school styles and the Quidditch uniforms reflected that aesthetic, combining nods to uniforms of several sports to create something she calls "timeless but familiar".

To that effect, the players wear long-sleeved crew-neck jumpers inspired by nineteenth-century fencing and tennis styles, incorporating their house colours. Their white trousers are also based on fencing garb. Worn over this is a short-sleeved robe that laces up at the front, also in house colours.

Quidditch padding is an amalgam of the protection used for polo and cricket. Heavily padded arm guards end over fingerless leather gloves. One-piece knee and shin guards, made of leather with a canvas lining and reinforced padded knees, buckle around thick, striped wool socks. The boots are similar to those worn when playing cricket.

Very few changes were made for *Harry Potter and the Chamber of Secrets*, the most noticeable one being that the robes were made in a lighter fabric for more flutter, to indicate faster flying speeds.

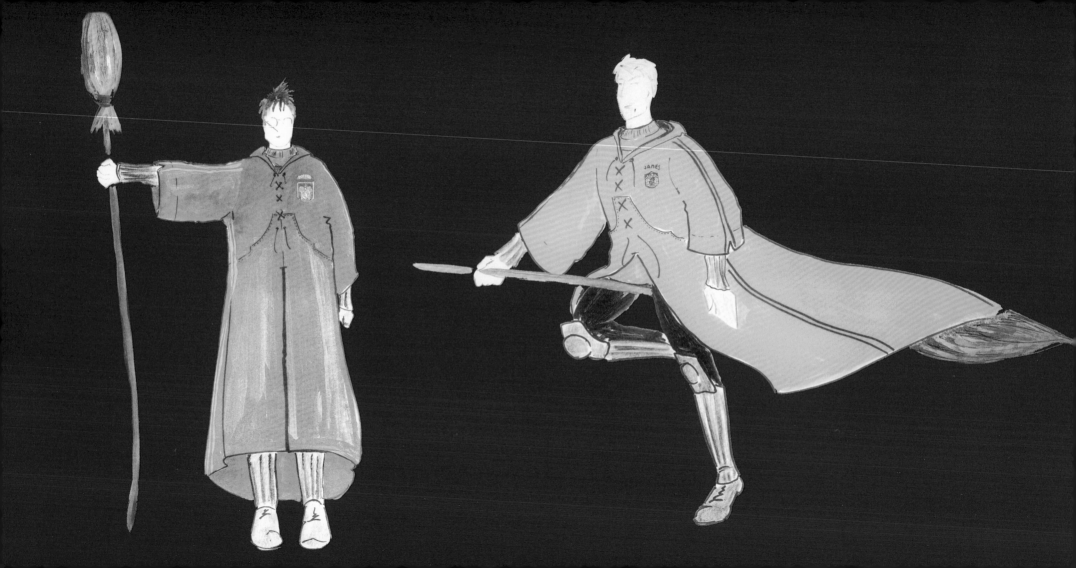

HOGWARTS QUIDDITCH UNIFORMS – YEAR THREE

In *Harry Potter and the Prisoner of Azkaban*, Gryffindor faces off against Hufflepuff during a driving rainstorm. This gave the film's new costume designer, Jany Temime, the opportunity to recreate the uniforms in a water-resistant nylon fabric, which immediately made the outfit contemporary. Goggles were added against the icy precipitation. Temime also added stripes, stars and most importantly, the name of the player on the back and sleeve of their robe, which she thought would make the uniform more relatable to teenage sports fans. "The idea was to modernise [the uniform] in such a way that kids who watch football or rugby will recognise Quidditch as being a sport they would play," she explains. And while watching it, "they could follow their favourite player." An identifying number for each player also appears on their robes, but initially the numbers were assigned randomly. Harry Potter wore number 7, which became every Seeker's number going forward.

The continually advancing technology of filming Quidditch allowed for bigger stunts and faster play. This required more comfort and safety for the actors harnessed to their broomsticks on the studio's green-screen set. In addition to the individually moulded bicycle seats added to their brooms, gussets were added to the Quidditch trouser seams to strengthen them. Even more comfort was achieved with padding added to the rear section of the Quidditch uniforms' trousers.

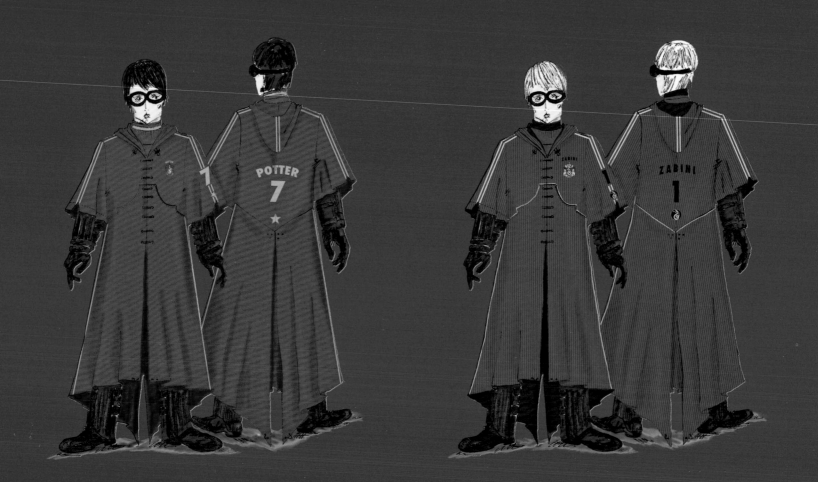

HOGWARTS QUIDDITCH UNIFORMS – YEAR SIX

Costume designer Jany Temime was excited when she learned that she would need to develop sportswear for Quidditch tryouts for *Harry Potter and the Half-Blood Prince*. Temime's idea was that the athletes should have something easy to put on, so underneath a sleeveless tunic that flares into a robe at the back, the players wear a dark grey, hooded warm-up suit. Each tunic has a number that corresponds to the seven positions in the game, and in theory, "you'd put on the number of the position you want," Temime explains. For *Half-Blood Prince* tryouts, it appears they've run out of the Keeper's number 1 tunics, as Ron Weasley and Cormac McLaggen wear 2 and 3, respectively, which are Beater numbers. Harry wears the Seeker's 7. Ginny Weasley wears the number 6 at tryouts, but after she makes the team she wears number 5 as one of the three Chasers.

As the aggressiveness of the game increased, Keepers needed to wear padded-leather chest and shoulder protectors and a padded helmet. The film-makers wanted Cormac McLaggen to appear much bigger than his competitor, Ron Weasley; however, actors Rupert Grint (Ron) and Freddie Stroma (Cormac) were roughly the same size. Extra panels were added to the padding Stroma wore, and his shoulder guards were scaled up to increase his size. Conversely, Grint wore padding and a helmet that were two sizes smaller than they should have been. His leather and laces were also scratched up with sandpaper to suggest the old, worn appearance of hand-me-downs.

QUIDDITCH PADDING – YEAR SIX

During his gruelling tryouts for Keeper, Ron Weasley ends up blocking the Quaffles thrown at him with his chest, foot and even his head. The game was rough and relentless, and so protective gear was amped up for hard, sustained play.

The new padding created for the Quidditch scenes in *Harry Potter and the Half-Blood Prince* drew from American football and Edwardian arm and leg guard designs, mostly made from thick moulded leather with a canvas lining which was stuffed with wadding. "The pads had to be very robust," says costume fabricator Steve Kill, "but also be flexible because the players are leaning forward on their broomsticks." In order to accommodate this position, shoulder and arm guards were crafted with multiple articulations. The majority of pieces were made to fit fifth-year through to seventh-year students, with one exception: a tinier version of the Quidditch padding was crafted for the character of Nigel Wolpert, who was in his third year at Hogwarts.

Right before the Quidditch tryouts scene was filmed, the film-makers suddenly decided they wanted to have a great pile of padding on the field that prospective players could try on, so a faster system of producing the items needed to be devised. "So, we reproduced them in a foam rubber plastic," explains Kill. "They took moulds off the leather and canvas pieces, and it was such a good moulding process that it picked up every little stitch." The non-leather padding was worn by background players as well as the stuntpeople, who preferred the lighter, more flexible rubber.

HOGWARTS FAN WEAR

Showing your team pride is paramount for fans of Quidditch, so the prop department provided plenty of paraphernalia for students to use when cheering on their house team. The graphics department designed banners and pennants fans could fly, as well as drums they could beat for each house.

In addition to creating tryout wear for potential Quidditch players in *Harry Potter and the Half-Blood Prince*, Jany Temime was also tasked with designing 'fan wear' for the students. Hoodies, T-shirts, wool hats and jogging bottoms, branded with the Hogwarts logo, were available in each of the house colours. Noticeably, Gryffindor supporters wear grey bottoms, and Slytherins, black.

Starting with the first film Temime worked on, *Harry Potter and the Prisoner of Azkaban*, a concerted effort was made to have the students be visually more modern and contemporary. As the students were becoming teenagers, it would be important for them to express their individuality through their clothes. Additionally, "Harry and Hermione are more aware of fashion in the Muggle world," she explains, and so their clothing choices should reflect that. Ron, Ginny and Luna would still be influenced by traditional wizard wear, but as teens would also be curious about current trends. "They live next to the Muggle world, they know what's happening there," she explains. "I wanted to dress them in a very cool way, but at the same time, of course, have something magical about it." Her only restriction was no Muggle brand names or logos on the apparel.

LUNA LOVEGOOD'S GRYFFINDOR LION HAT

"You look dreadful, Ron."

Luna Lovegood, *Harry Potter and the Half-Blood Prince*

In *Harry Potter and the Half-Blood Prince*, Ravenclaw Luna Lovegood demonstrates her support for her friends on the Gryffindor Quidditch team by wearing a large lion-shaped hat. Visual development artist Adam Brockbank drew up a range of possible designs for the hat, but it was actually actress Evanna Lynch, who plays Luna, that offered a key piece of input on the headpiece, asking if it could look as if the lion was eating her head. The hat is very subtly animated – it blinks and moves its eyes to follow the direction of the conversation between Luna, Harry, Ron, Hermione and Ginny.

   "The best thing about playing Luna," says Lynch, "is that when you're wearing her clothes, which no one would wear in their right mind, you get out of yourself and you're very free. The lion hat was intensely like, 'I can't care what anyone thinks, I'm wearing a lion hat on my head.' It was very light and comfortable; I kept forgetting I was wearing it, even though people were looking at me. It was a lot of fun."

FILMING QUIDDITCH – THE EARLY YEARS

The Quidditch match sequences in the Harry Potter films have a look and excitement comparable to any high-speed, fast-moving, action-packed sport. To accomplish this, the moves for each game were planned in advance and tested out by the stunt crew. Additionally, an animated version of the match, known as a 'pre-viz' (for pre-visualisation), was created to assess how the necessary elements – the Scottish Highlands mountains in the background, towers and spectators, the moves of Quaffles, Bludgers and the Snitch – needed to be composited for the completed scene.

Only when all of this pre-production work was done were the actors shot – one at a time – on a studio set covered in blue-screen material and lined with pads for everyone's safety. For the earliest filming, each actor would be suspended up to ten feet in the air from a rigging of wires or sit on a computer-controlled rig arm pre-programmed with tilting and turning moves. The process was incredibly time-consuming: a two-second shot that featured ten players might involve a week's worth of filming, after which the visual effects team would begin their work.

In *Harry Potter and the Philosopher's Stone*, Harry's broom is jinxed and he ends up hanging from the handle as it tries to shake him off. For this stunt, Daniel Radcliffe (Harry) hung from a broomstick suspended twenty-two feet high. "I was wired up to the broom," says Radcliffe, "with a huge airbag underneath me, and they moved me around up there. That was brilliant!"

Fortunately, as the film series progressed, the technology behind broom-flying advanced too, as did the comfort of the actors. The Quidditch match that occurs in *Harry Potter and the Prisoner of Azkaban* sees Harry challenged by inclement weather and a confrontation with Dementors. Developments in computer technology enabled the film-makers to create digital doubles of the actors, and these computer-generated versions of the cast could perform moves that might be impossible for the most talented of athletes.

FILMING QUIDDITCH – YEAR SIX

Harry becomes captain of the Gryffindor Quidditch team in *Harry Potter and the Half-Blood Prince*. As many players have graduated from Hogwarts (or left, as did the Weasley twins), he holds tryouts for new team members, including new Chasers and a new Keeper. These positions are desired, respectively, by a proactive Ginny Weasley and a hopeful, yet doubtful, Ron Weasley.

As the players matured, the game became wilder and the stunts became bigger. New systems were installed in the blue-screen sets, such as a large motion-base rig that could move up and down while at the same time rotating 360 degrees both horizontally and vertically. A wire-grid system was added to the studio ceiling, which allowed even more horizontal, vertical and angled movements. Finally, there was a large mounted swing that literally allowed the stuntpeople to fly in free fall. As the swing moved back and forth, a stuntperson on a broom could launch into the air up to twenty feet high and 'fly' for forty feet.

In addition to breathtaking stunts, the film-makers also wanted to give audiences the feeling that the Quidditch game was being filmed in the same way as a televised Muggle sport, with its multiple moving camera angles, and so the visual effects team presented the action as if viewed by a flying cameraman. To add to the effect, the snow that falls during the match appears to hit the camera lens as it follows the action.

PROFESSIONAL QUIDDITCH AND THE 422ND QUIDDITCH WORLD CUP

I N *HARRY POTTER AND THE GOBLET OF FIRE*, Harry is invited by the Weasleys to attend the finals of the 422nd Quidditch World Cup – the greatest magical event of the year. They're joined by Hufflepuff student Cedric Diggory and his father, before being whisked off to the stadium grounds by Portkey.

The arrival in the stadium of the finalists for the World Cup is impressive and fantastic. Ireland arrive first, setting off fireworks that transform into a dancing leprechaun. The Irish National Quidditch Team fly in on brooms that evoke the Nimbus 2000 style, made from a rich brown wood with a long bristle head. The Bulgarian National Quidditch Team shoot into the stadium through the leprechaun, extinguishing it, then let their dynamic Seeker take the stage. The Bulgarian team's brooms have very dark bristle heads with a small uplift at the end.

The graphics department created the teams' logos, seen on an assortment of Quidditch World Cup ephemera that any fan would covet, including posters, pins and badges for both the Irish and Bulgarian teams. The official programme features team profiles and a chart of their formations, plus a list of the event's sponsors. Memorabilia was also created for other Quidditch teams, such as the Holyhead Harpies and Ron Weasley's favourites, the Chudley Cannons.

VIKTOR KRUM'S BROOM

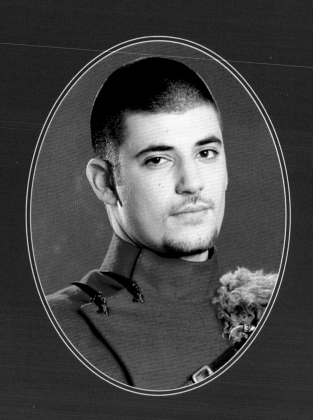

"That, sis, is the best Seeker in the world. Krum!"

Fred Weasley, *Harry Potter and the Goblet of Fire*

The Seeker for the Bulgarian team at the 422nd Quidditch World Cup is Durmstrang Institute student Viktor Krum. Durmstrang is one of the two wizarding schools that visit Hogwarts for the Triwizard Tournament in *Harry Potter and the Goblet of Fire*, and Krum is chosen as the champion for the magical competition. "He is a worldwide hero," says Stanislav Ianevski, who plays Krum, "because he's the best Seeker; he flies the best way with his broom. He's sort of worshipped by other players, as we see in the film, but he's really a nice guy."

"We designed a special broomstick for Krum," says concept artist Adam Brockbank, "although Quidditch moves so quickly, you might not notice it. It was more streamlined than most and quite flat on top with a spine underneath." The top and bottom were in different colours; the lacquered top matched the red of the Bulgarian team uniform. The underside of the broom, which was constructed in rubber, was a light brown but could reflect the red of Krum's uniform depending on the lighting. The foot pedals were made of a thick bronze metal.

After Krum flies in with this team, he catches the crowd's attention by flipping his broom backwards and performing a handstand on the handle, similar to performing a freestyle motocross trick. No seat on the broom is seen, as the move was created digitally.

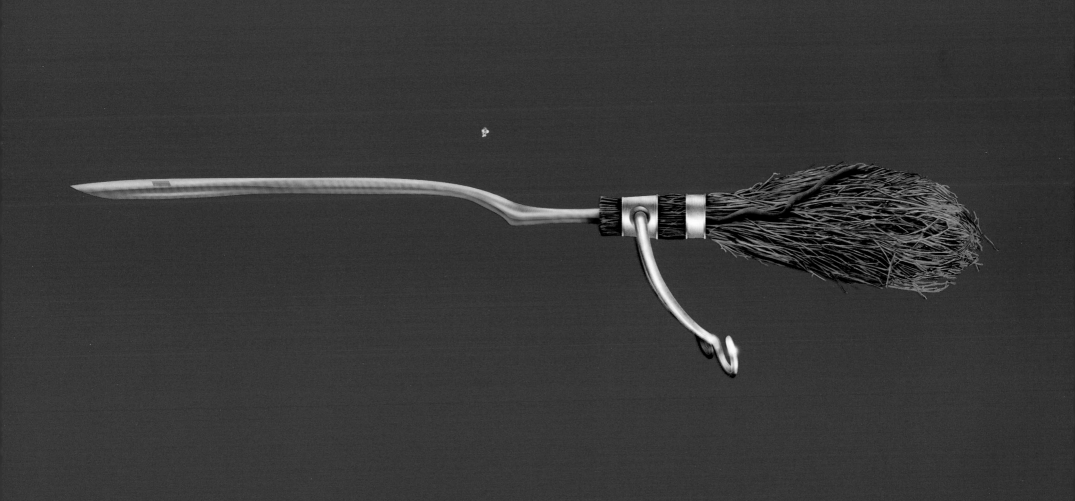

QUIDDITCH WORLD CUP UNIFORMS

Costume designer Jany Temime applied her redesign of the Hogwarts Quidditch uniforms for *Harry Potter and the Prisoner of Azkaban* to the two teams competing in the final of the Quidditch World Cup, as seen in *Harry Potter and the Goblet of Fire*. The robes of both the Irish and Bulgarian sides are made from a light material and bear the team's logo on the front, the name of the team member on the back and their position number on the back and left sleeve. Padding for the players is made from very thick moulded leather.

Temime also provided attire for souvenir sellers and team supporters. Merchandise vendors at the World Cup campsite sport team colours and easily spotted hats inspired by medieval fool's caps. Fans also wear distinctive headwear, including top hats and bowlers. The Weasleys (except for Ron) and Hermione show their Irish pride – Ron and Harry cheer for Bulgaria.

-BULGARIAN TEAM-

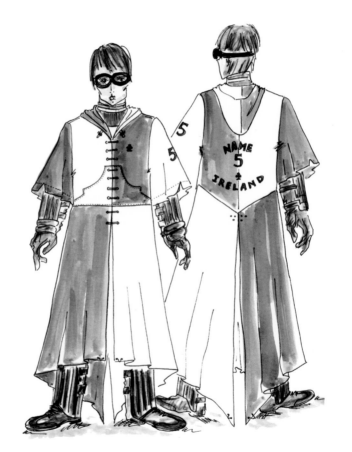

-IRISH TEAM-

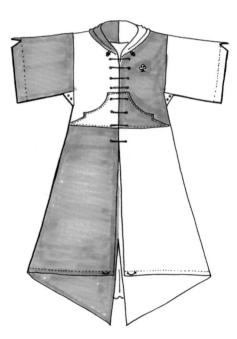

PROFESSIONAL QUIDDITCH BOOKS AND MEDIA

Fans of professional Quidditch teams can follow their favourites in *Seeker Weekly*, the international Quidditch magazine printed in the UK, which was actually designed and written by graphic artists Miraphora Mina and Eduardo Lima. This issue would not please Ron Weasley, as his beloved team, the Chudley Cannons, is in danger of being sent down to become a minor team in the ranks. An article comparing two new brooms – the Air Wave Gold and the Turbo XXX – is advertised on the front cover; pumpkin juice is advertised on the back.

Books about Quidditch are popular with the students, one being *Quidditch Teams of England and Ireland*, written by Miro Limus, a portmanteau of the two graphic artists' names. Another book features the Chudley Cannons exclusively – *Flying with the Cannons* – an essential book for every Chudley Cannons fan. This commemorative edition '[exalts] the Cannons' glorious past, present & future'. For publications not mentioned specifically in J.K. Rowling's novels, the graphics team wrote all cover copy and entries, subject to the author's approval.

Additional ephemera for Chudley Cannons fans included posters and insignia. One poster proclaims the Chudley Cannons' motto: Let's All Just Keep Our Fingers Crossed and Hope for the Best!

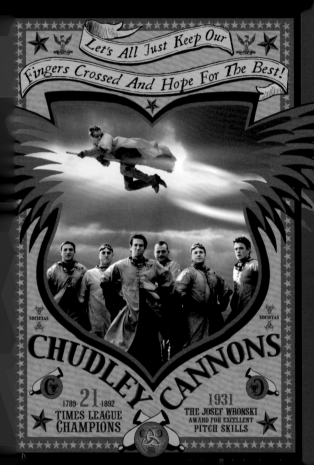

Let's All Just Keep Our

Fingers Crossed And Hope For The Best!

SOCIETAS

SOCIETAS

CHUDLEY CANNONS

21
1789-1892
TIMES LEAGUE
CHAMPIONS

1931
THE JOSEF WRONSKI
AWARD FOR EXCELLENT
PITCH SKILLS

HOLYHEAD HARPIES

HOLYHEAD HARPIES FOUNDED IN 1203

FLYING WITH THE CANNONS

A COMMEMORATIVE BOOK EXAMINING
THE CHUDLEY CANNONS
MAIDEN PASSIONATE JOURNEY A LIFETIME

written by Janus Brholt

Q.U.A.B.B.L.E.
QUIDDITCH
teams of
ENGLAND
IRELAND
Miro Limus

An
EXTRAORDINARY
visual record
of the ART of
QUIDDITCH

QUIDDITCH
teams of
ENGLAND &
IRELAND

Q.U.A.B.B.L.E.
QUIDDITCH
teams of
ENGLAND &
IRELAND
Miro Limus

REVISED
EDITION
with a new preface by
Lucas Clepsley

MERGO

MERGO

MERGO

Venus in PISCES · Ed. 240274

SEEKER WEEKLY
INTERNATIONAL QUIDDITCH MAGAZINE
PRINTED IN THE UK

WHICH BROOM?

TURBO XXX

Air Wave Gold

Vs.

**CHUDLEY CANNONS
FACE RELEGATION!**

100 TICKETS
UP FOR GRABS

PRIDE OF PORTREE
Vs.
FALMOUTH FALCONS
SEE INSIDE FOR
MORE DETAILS

**CORRUPTION IN
THE QUIDDITCH
LEAGUE:**

**HOW THE TORNADOS
ARE TAKING CONTROL**

QUIDDITCH MEMORABILIA

After the 422nd Quidditch World Cup ended, memorabilia of the Irish National Team can be seen on Seamus Finnigan's bedside table in the Gryffindor boys' dormitory, in *Harry Potter and the Goblet of Fire*. Another Gryffindor roommate, the Muggle-born Dean Thomas, decorated his area with memorabilia for England's West Ham United Football Club. Ron Weasley, of course, has a Chudley Cannons poster and other mementos next to his bed at Hogwarts.

At The Burrow, the Weasley home, Ron's bedroom continues his tribute to his favourite team. There is another Chudley Cannons poster tacked to his wall, but perhaps his best keepsake is an orange-striped Afghan bedspread featuring the Cannons' logo, seen in *Harry Potter and the Goblet of Fire* when Hermione wakes Ron and Harry to get going for the Quidditch World Cup. Set designer Stephenie McMillan decided that as Molly Weasley, Ron's mother, was a great knitter, his bed should have a knitted cover. McMillan had an on-site knitter, Shirley Lancaster, who created the sweaters the Weasley siblings received each Christmas and the patchwork blanket on Ron's dormitory bed, among other items. "So, Shirley knitted a huge orange bedcover with the word *Chudley* appliquéd on it, and a flying Quidditch player, for his favourite team, which is quite spectacular," says McMillan.

The bedcover is seen again in *Harry Potter and the Half-Blood Prince*, when Harry and Hermione join the Weasleys at The Burrow before school starts. "Sadly, due to the burning down of The Burrow," she continues, "it couldn't be seen again in the films, but it'll be kept as a gem, I'm sure."

BROOM BROOM *kit*

Bling up your broom!

L. Wakefield's
BROOMCARE
WAX
QUIDDITCH
SUPPLIES
200 g NET WT 7.05 OZ

BROOMSTICK SERVICING KIT

BROOM CARE

Brooms go through a lot of wear and tear, and so broom care products are essential for broom riders. Weasleys' Wizard Wheezes offers a Broom Broom kit that will help you 'bling up your broom!' designed by the graphics department, headed by Miraphora Mina and Eduardo Lima, with the assistance of Lauren Wakefield. One kitted-out broom has fireworks attached to the tip of the handle and underneath the seat, and a drag foil sitting on top of the bristle-head branches.

Mina and Lima often used family and crew member names on the products, and Wakefield gets a callout on a package for Broomcare Wax, more than likely sold at Quality Quidditch Supplies in Diagon Alley.

SNITCH SNATCHER!

Snitch Snatcher! (The Quidditch Game) is a board game version of the wizarding world's favourite sport. The game is played in the Great Hall by Fred and George Weasley in a scene deleted from *Harry Potter and the Prisoner of Azkaban*. Graphic designers Miraphora Mina and Eduardo Lima crafted a cardboard miniature of a Quidditch pitch, with player game pieces that can be 'flown' over the game board by sitting them atop handheld 'brooms.' A sheet of cut-out-and-assemble spectator towers is provided, all in the Hogwarts house colours.

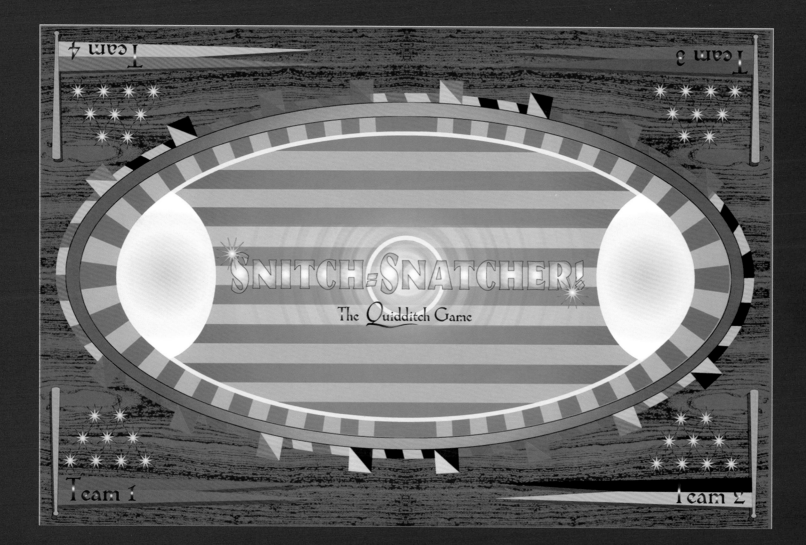

THE ORDER OF THE PHOENIX

D URING THE FIRST WIZARDING WAR, Albus Dumbledore assembled a group of wizards and witches dedicated to vanquishing the Dark Lord Voldemort, who then disappeared after he tried to kill Harry Potter with the Killing Curse, *Avada Kedavra*. When Voldemort returns to corporeal form in *Harry Potter and the Goblet of Fire*, the Order is reestablished with new and former members.

In *Harry Potter and the Order of the Phoenix*, five members of the Order – Alastor 'Mad-Eye' Moody, Kingsley Shacklebolt, Nymphadora Tonks, Emmeline Vance and Elphias Doge – come to Privet Drive to provide Harry with a protective escort to the Order's headquarters at number twelve, Grimmauld Place. The Order members fly along the River Thames to reach their destination, and so new brooms needed to be created for the characters.

Other than Daniel Radcliffe, none of the other actors had 'flown' on brooms before. "It's a difficult environment and a long process," second unit director Stephen Woolfenden explains. "They're being blasted with three or four wind machines, they can't hear anything, and they need to learn the moves and make them look natural." Peter Cartwright, who plays Elphias Doge, was seventy-one years old at the time. "We just needed to be careful about how long we [kept] him up on the rig," Woolfenden says, "but he was absolutely fantastic and told us, 'This is one of the most amazing filming days of my life.' He did two or three days up on there and was very, very good."

ALASTOR 'MAD-EYE' MOODY'S BROOM

"We have to use those means of transport the trace can't detect. Brooms, Thestrals, and the like."

Alastor Moody, *Harry Potter and the Deathly Hallows – Part 1*

Harry Potter and the Order of the Phoenix is the first time Harry meets the real Alastor Moody, who is in charge of his transfer to Grimmauld Place. Moody is dressed in a 'gunslinger-style' coat, which inspired concept artist Adam Brockbank's antihero design for his broom. "I went to Stuart Craig with an idea for an *Easy Rider* broom for Moody, where he would sit with his legs forward, like a motorcycle," recalls Brockbank. By the final version, "it was a really cool broom," he continues. "It was beautifully made, and you can see by the way he sits in it that it's different from the others."

The broom is crafted from a mahogany-coloured wood with flowing curves and pedals set at the front that give it the look of a chopper. While the 'seat' of the broom is hidden under Moody's coat, the broom has a seat back that he leans on and handheld steering controls. The bristle head is a tight cluster of straw-coloured branches, and the back of the seat folds up for easy carrying.

"I have the coolest broom in the cupboard," actor Brendan Gleeson (Moody) says with a laugh. "This is the broomstick of all broomsticks as far as I'm concerned." Gleeson admits that, at the best of times, he didn't like heights, but he does love speed, and found filming the flying sequence great fun, "like a fairground ride."

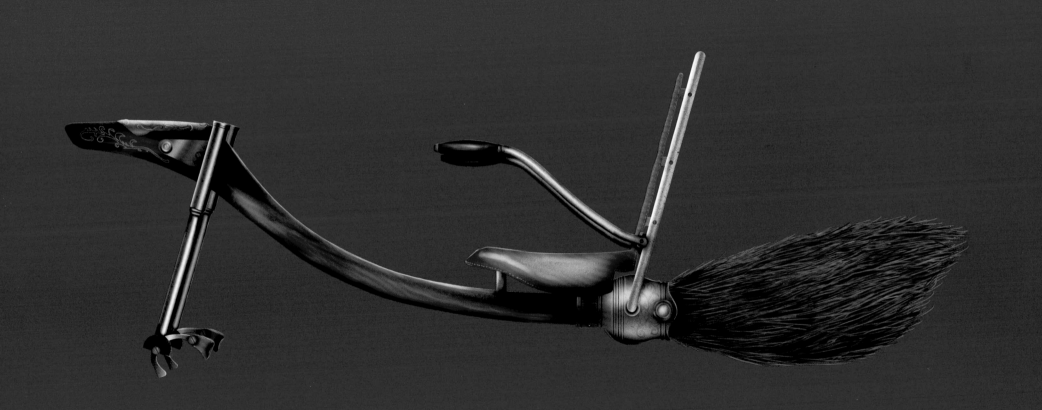

KINGSLEY SHACKLEBOLT'S BROOM

"Kinglsey, you take point."

Alastor Moody, *Harry Potter and the Order of the Phoenix*

Kingsley Shacklebolt is a member of the Order of the Phoenix while, at the same time, he is employed at the Ministry of Magic as an Auror. In *Harry Potter and the Order of the Phoenix*, he is part of the quintet that flies Harry from Privet Drive to number twelve, Grimmauld Place, the Order's headquarters.

Actor George Harris, who plays the double agent, loved the flying sequences and wished he could have done more of them. Costume designer Jany Temime had dressed him in a long, heavy gown, "and you know we had a lot of wind around us [while flying]," says Harris. "That definitely enhanced the look of it."

Shacklebolt's broom has a long, straight bristle head made out of a different material than most other brooms. It also appears to utilise savannah grasses for a wrapped decoration around the bristle head. The handle is a mottled, bent branch with a smaller branch shooting off, which could be used as a handhold if desired. There are also two thick brass collars on the head, but its pedals are delicate, with rounded tips.

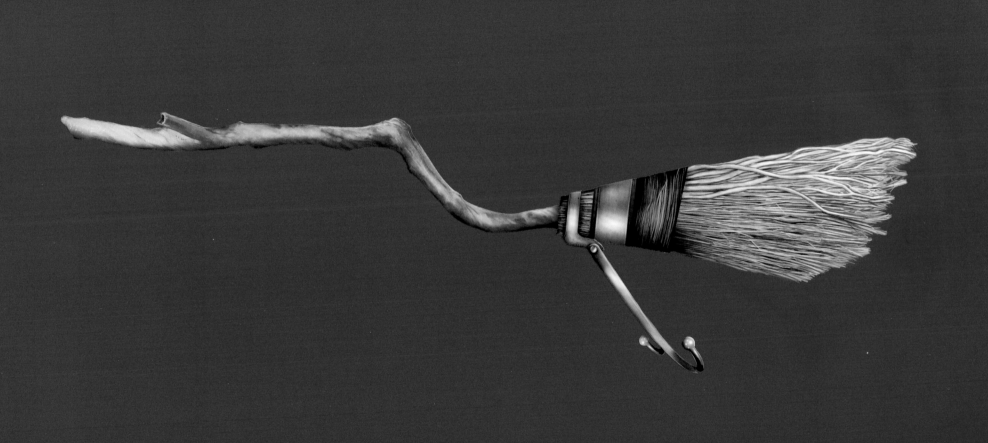

NYMPHADORA TONKS'S BROOM

"Don't call me Nymphadora!"

Tonks, *Harry Potter and the Order of the Phoenix*

Nymphadora Tonks is a young Auror at the Ministry of Magic, under the tutelage of Alastor Moody, who joins the second Order of the Phoenix. She was born a Metamorphmagus, meaning she can change her physical appearance at will, and her hair changes colour frequently – to purple or orange or white – depending on her mood. The broom makers took their cue from her palette and added different coloured branches inside the bristle head of her broom. Its pedals are silver, and a silver band holds a leather cover, like a fender, over the top of the bristle head. The handle is made from a dark wood with burls and knobs layered through its rough bark. Finally, Tonks has tied a a pair of thin purple and pink ribbons around the top.

"I think everyone should get on a broomstick," says Natalia Tena, who plays Tonks. "Until I was six, I believed three witches had left me at the doorstep. On my eighteenth birthday, my mother gave me a broom, so perhaps this was meant to be." Tena was an avid broomstick flyer, loving the height and movement of the hydraulic rig. "The first time I did it, it took thirty-six takes to do it right because I was giggling so much," says Tena. "I was just having so much fun." She also loved the 'manky' look of her broom. "I know everyone wanted to take their wands with them at the end of shooting," she says, "but I wanted my broomstick."

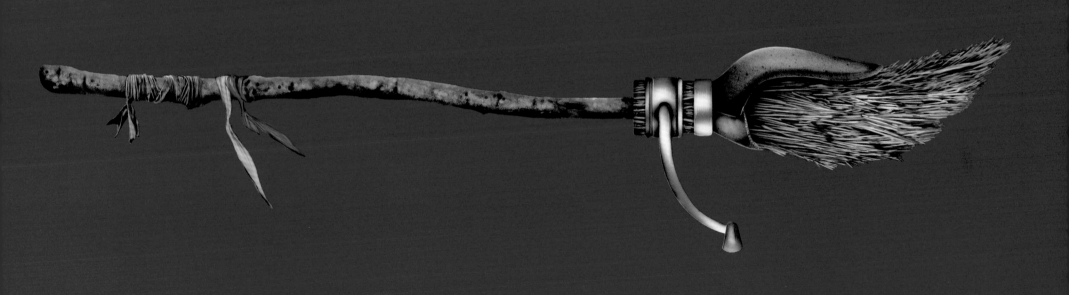

BATTLE OF
THE SEVEN POTTERS

HARRY POTTER'S SAFETY FROM VOLDEMORT and his Death Eaters is paramount in *Harry Potter and the Deathly Hallows – Part 1*, and so the Order of the Phoenix demands that he leave the suburban home of his aunt and uncle and take refuge at The Burrow. However, being under seventeen, Harry still has the 'trace' on him, so a unique subterfuge is devised: using Polyjuice Potion, there are six additional 'Harrys' who fly in different directions to thwart his pursuers.

Bill Weasley and Fleur Delacour (disguised as Harry) fly on a Thestral, as do Hermione Granger (Harry) and Kingsley Shacklebolt. The real Harry Potter flies alongside Hagrid, in a sidecar attached to his motorcycle. Needless to say, the majority use brooms: Tonks with Ron (Harry), Remus and George (Harry), and Arthur and Fred (Harry). Sharp eyes may notice that one of the disguised Harrys is flying Harry's Firebolt. Mad-Eye Moody is accompanied by reluctant Order member Mundungus Fletcher (Harry), who disapparates at the first sign of trouble.

Once aloft, the Order is attacked by Death Eaters in a spectacular aerial battle. "When we started on the films, the only way we could get the power we needed to control broomstick rigs was by hydraulic pumps and rams," says special effects supervisor John Richardson. By the time of the seventh film, an all-electronic system was in place that could manoeuvre complex axis setups and rigs, controlled by a program that perfectly interfaced with pre-visualisations the visual effects department had devised. "The technology was now there for us to use," he adds, "and we've taken full advantage of it."

HAGRID'S MOTORCYCLE

When Rubeus Hagrid brings the infant Harry Potter to his aunt's house on Privet Drive after his parents are killed by Voldemort, in *Harry Potter and the Philosopher's Stone*, he flies not on a broom but on a 1959 Triumph Bonneville T120 motorcycle. Seventeen years later, in *Harry Potter and the Deathly Hallows – Part 1*, Hagrid takes Harry Potter away from Privet Drive using the same form of transportation, though the motorcycle this time is a robin's-egg blue Royal Enfield with a Watsonian sidecar.

"We tried to match the iconic motorbike used in *Philosopher's Stone*, but it was difficult to get hold of," says John Richardson, "so we found a similar-looking bike that was readily available." Seven matching motorcycles were needed to film the sequence: two had an upgraded engine installed for stunt work, and the others were rebuilt for wire and crane work with motorised wheels that would spin when lifted in the air.

During their escape, Hagrid drives the motorcycle into a tunnel, then manoeuvres it up the wall and upside down, nearly dumping Harry out of the sidecar. Another motorcycle was retrofitted with straps and moulded fibreglass seats strong enough to hold in a stuntman wearing a full-size Hagrid costume. Background plates and right-side-up stunts were filmed in Liverpool's Queensway Tunnel.

Finally, the motorbike makes a crash-landing into the marsh surrounding The Burrow, a stunt achieved by sending another rebuilt Royal Enfield down a track into a water-filled set, akin to a log-flume ride.

ARTHUR WEASLEY'S BROOM

"Are we the last back? Where's George?"

Arthur Weasley, *Harry Potter and the Deathly Hallows – Part 1*

The Weasley parents, Molly and Arthur, are members of the Second Order of the Phoenix, and Arthur participates in the subterfuge of transferring Harry Potter from Privet Drive to The Burrow, the Weasleys' home, in *Harry Potter and the Deathly Hallows – Part 1*. For this ride, the patriarch of the family shares his broom with his son Fred.

Arthur Weasley's broom was designed by graphic artist Miraphora Mina, who was often asked to design props. It exemplifies his love of Muggle artefacts: instead of a footrest, the pedals are actual bicycle pedals, the seat is also from a bicycle, and it even has a basket on the back of the seat. The broom's bristle head is made from decidedly orange branches.

Thought was given to completely redesigning the brooms that would need to accommodate two wizards, but it was decided to keep the one-person design intact and have the second person sit behind the broom-flyer – as you would with two passengers on one bicycle.

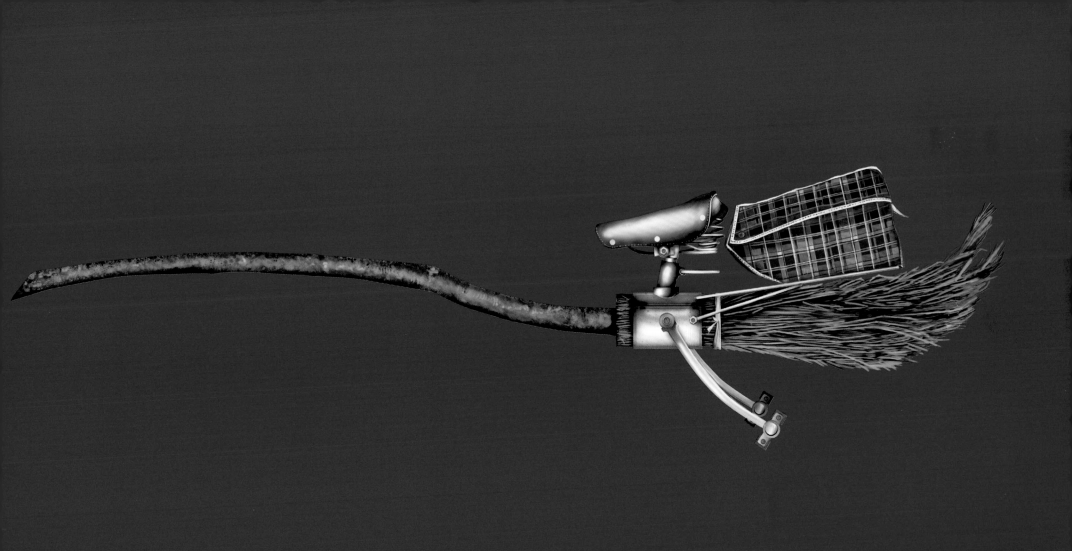

REMUS LUPIN'S BROOM

"What creature sat in the corner the first time Harry Potter visited my office in Hogwarts?"

Remus Lupin, *Harry Potter and the Deathly Hallows – Part 1*

Remus Lupin was a friend of Harry Potter's father, James, and became Defence Against the Dark Arts professor at Hogwarts in Harry's third year, during the events of *Harry Potter and the Prisoner of Azkaban*. Lupin was a member of the original Order and continued his fight with the Second Order of the Phoenix. As such, Lupin takes part in moving Harry from Privet Drive to The Burrow in *Harry Potter and the Deathly Hallows – Part 1*, to keep him safe from attacking Death Eaters.

Lupin's broom reflects his own impoverished state, as his life and work have been marked by his lycanthropy, which has led him to a life of impermanence and poverty. His broom is made from a light-coloured wood, smoothed out for the most part, although the tip appears broken off. A brass collar holds together the bristle head, which reflects the circumstances of its flyer; its branches are extremely thin and almost resemble matted fur rather than twigs.

Actor David Thewlis, who plays Lupin, looked forward to flying on a broom after he read the script for *Deathly Hallows – Part 1*, especially as he was one of the last actors to 'fly'. "Like turning into a werewolf, it was something you could say you've done," says Thewlis. "There were so many things in this film you could go back to your family and go, 'Guess what I did today?' and it was really cool to be able to tell my little girl, 'I was on a broomstick today'."

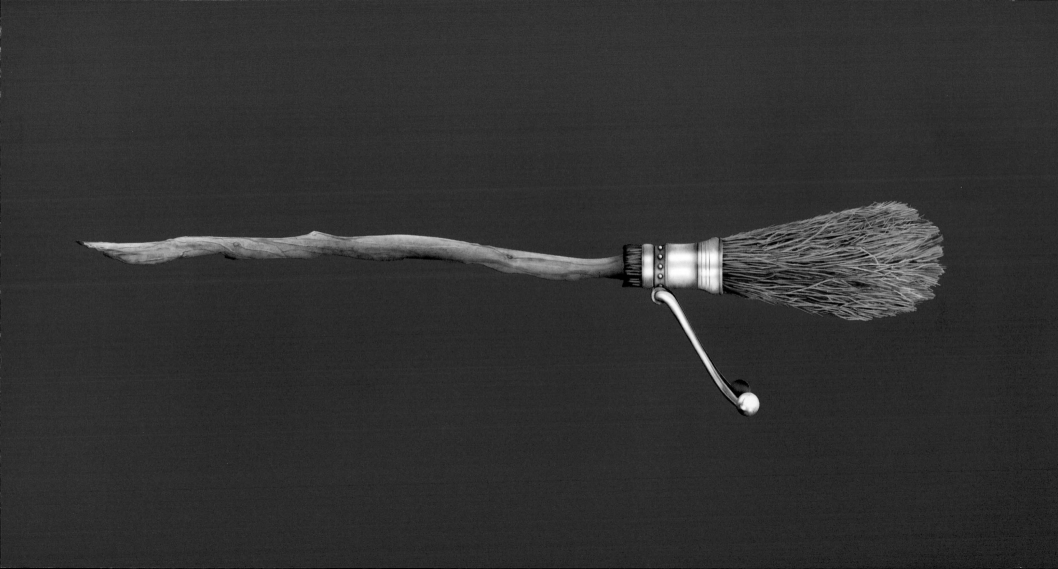

DEATH EATER BROOMS

Almost immediately after taking flight from Privet Drive, Harry Potter and his protectors from the Order of the Phoenix are surrounded by Death Eaters – fervent followers of Voldemort – who then quickly begin one-on-one attacks. Three Death Eaters peel off and pursue Hagrid and Harry, following them as Hagrid hits a power booster on his motorcycle and heads to escape through a tunnel. Harry manages to knock one away and another is removed by out-of-control traffic. But before they can exit the tunnel, the third Death Eater renders Hagrid unconscious. Taking over the controls, Harry struggles to elude their pursuer, who is finally thrown off-balance by Harry's owl, Hedwig.

The design of the Death Eaters' brooms is streamlined and efficient. The shaft of the broomstick, made with ebony-coloured wood, curves in a gentle arc. Its neatly trimmed bristles are also black, and its pedals and collar match the oxidized silver of the Firebolt design. The ferrule, or pommel, of the broom was also cast in silver, with blackened ornamentation. "The Death Eaters generally have quite showy aesthetics," says art director Hattie Storey, "with their masks made out of filigreed silver. Their costumes are quite intricate, as well." And so it made sense to bring this aesthetic to the Death Eater brooms on the one place that wouldn't be covered by robes.

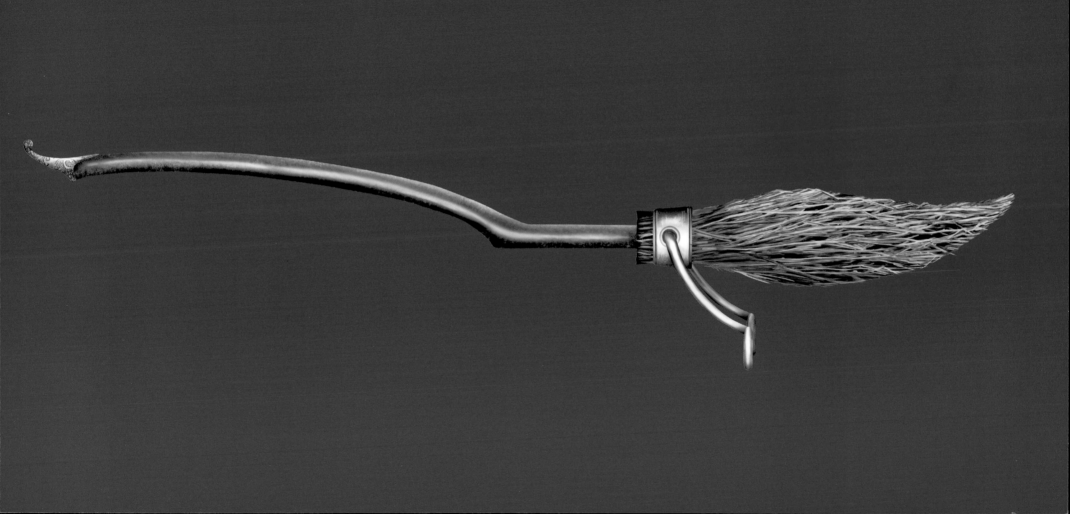

ESCAPE FROM
THE ROOM OF REQUIREMENT

BROOMS IN THE ROOM OF REQUIREMENT

Throughout the events of *Harry Potter and the Deathly Hallows – Parts 1* and *2*, Harry, Ron and Hermione search furtively for the seven Horcruxes Voldemort has created in order to become immortal, so that they can destroy them. By questioning the ghost of Rowena Ravenclaw's daughter, Helena, Harry learns that one Horcrux – the Ravenclaw diadem – is hidden in the Room of Requirement.

The diadem is recovered, but as the trio try to leave they are stopped by Draco Malfoy, flanked by his cronies Gregory Goyle and Blaise Zabini. When Goyle ineptly casts a Fiendfyre Curse and cannot control the flames, it is a dash to find a way out. Suddenly, when Ron is cast back by the fire, he stumbles into a cache of disparate brooms that have been stored in the Room of Requirement.

Those brooms have a variety of styles – some complex, some simple. Ron tosses Harry a broom that has triangular filigreed stirrups and a recurved handle made from highly polished dark wood. Ron's broom handle is straight, with a brass cap on its tip and bicycle pedals. Hermione's broom has a Firebolt-shaped body.

The scene in the Room of Requirement is the only time Hermione Granger rides on a broom in the films. As she shouts while riding Buckbeak the Hippogriff to help Sirius Black escape in *Harry Potter and the Prisoner of Azkaban*: "I don't like flying!"

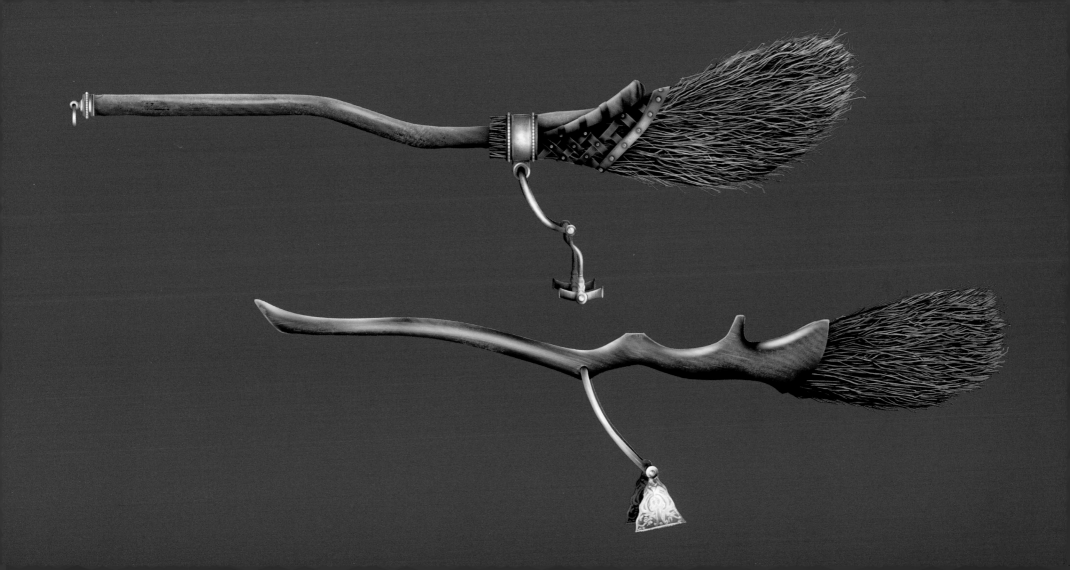

FLEEING FIENDFYRE

As Fiendfyre rages in the Room of Requirement, Draco Malfoy and Blaise Zabini become trapped atop burning towers of desks and chairs. (Gregory Goyle has fallen into the flames.) Harry knows he can't leave them there, so he turns around to rescue them. Ron follows reluctantly, declaring, "If we die for them, Harry, I'll kill you!" Harry takes Draco, Ron takes Blaise, and they race after Hermione, who has cleared a path out of the room. This was the first time in the Harry Potter films that brooms needed to hold two riders while performing complicated stunt work.

The double-passenger brooms were called 'the rescue rig' by the special effects crew. This rig was mounted on a track so it could be flown at high speeds to achieve the stunt. "The flier on the broom had to link arms with the guy on the table and swing him on to the back of the broom, cowboy-style," says John Richardson. "That was tricky to work out, but I think it came out great."

Once the students escape the Fiendfyre, they must land. "The challenge is it's a real-time stunt, it's a real impact on the floor," explains Stephen Woolfenden. "And it's using a broomstick that's going to get entwined with them." In front of a green screen, two stuntmen straddled Harry's broom while standing on a platform on a track that was pushed to quickly accelerate forward. As the rig hit a designated point and came to a stop, the stuntmen jumped off and crash-landed on the floor.

THE BROOMS OF FANTASTIC BEASTS

The events of *Fantastic Beasts: The Crimes of Grindelwald* take place in the 1920s, as the Dark wizard Gellert Grindelwald escalates his campaign to create a ruling class of pure-blood wizards. Arrested in New York by the Magical Congress of the United States (MACUSA), he needs to be transferred to the Ministry of Magic in London to be brought to trial. The prisoner's Thestral-driven carriage is followed by a security team of four Aurors on broomsticks. For these brooms, production design wanted a model that would appear fast and efficient. "It would be like the police car equivalent of a broomstick," says concept artist Molly Sole. "And it's got to look like it's moving. So, we created a broom that was older looking in style, but with an edgier, more speedy design." The handle was cast in polyurethane resin, then long wood twigs were applied one by one to create the broom head.

When Grindelwald hijacks the carriage, the Aurors are blasted away by lightning strikes conjured by the escaped wizard. "We tried to reinvent broom flying for this," says assistant stunt coordinator Marc Mailley. Instead of motion-control bases, the team used a counterbalance rig held up by wires called a tuning fork. As there is no equipment underneath the riders in this system, cameras could film lower angles and closer passes than before. "And instead of being led by the broom, the rider actually leads the broom," explains Mailley. "It's probably as close to riding a broomstick without physically being able to do it."

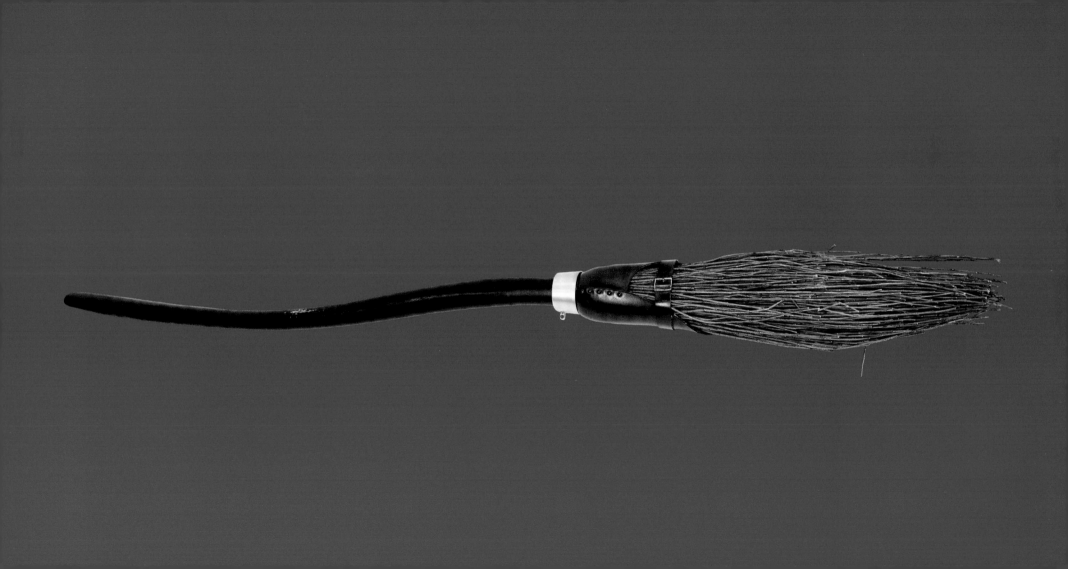

PLACE CACHÉE BROOMS

Fantastic Beasts: The Crimes of Grindelwald takes place in both London and Paris, so the film-makers were given the challenge of creating merchandise for the French equivalent of Diagon Alley – known as the Place Cachée. Production designer Stuart Craig and set decorator Anna Pinnock knew this wizarding marketplace should contain shops similar to the ones in Diagon Alley that provide necessities for the students of Hogwarts. There is a cauldron store called Monsieur Sanfin Chaudrons, the apothecary Dr Aziz Branchiflore, the Maison Capenoir for robes and the shop of Gaston McAaron that sells Quidditch supplies.

Gaston McAaron's offers the items needed for the wizarding world's favourite sport – Quaffles, Bludgers and, of course, brooms – with a French flair. The film's story takes place in 1927 – a time when the art nouveau style of naturalistic design was prevalent. This became the inspiration for all of the Quidditch supplies.

The curves of the broom's silver handle are asymmetrical, with a flow that echoes natural shapes and forms, such as the graceful coil of a plant or the sinuous neck of a bird. The materials in the broom head are lighter and sharper than other brooms, almost resembling porcupine quills, bound by three braided natural wraps.

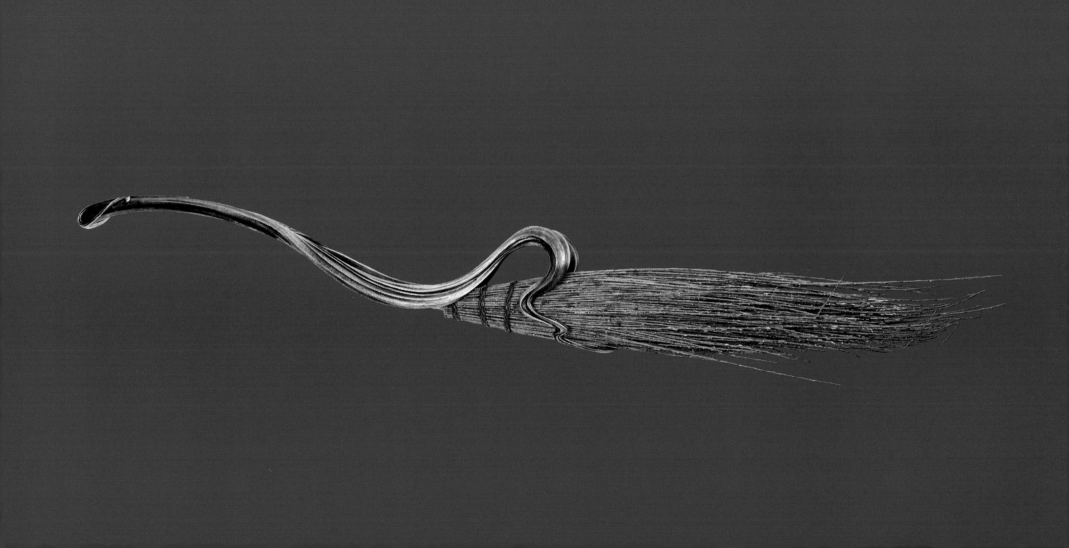

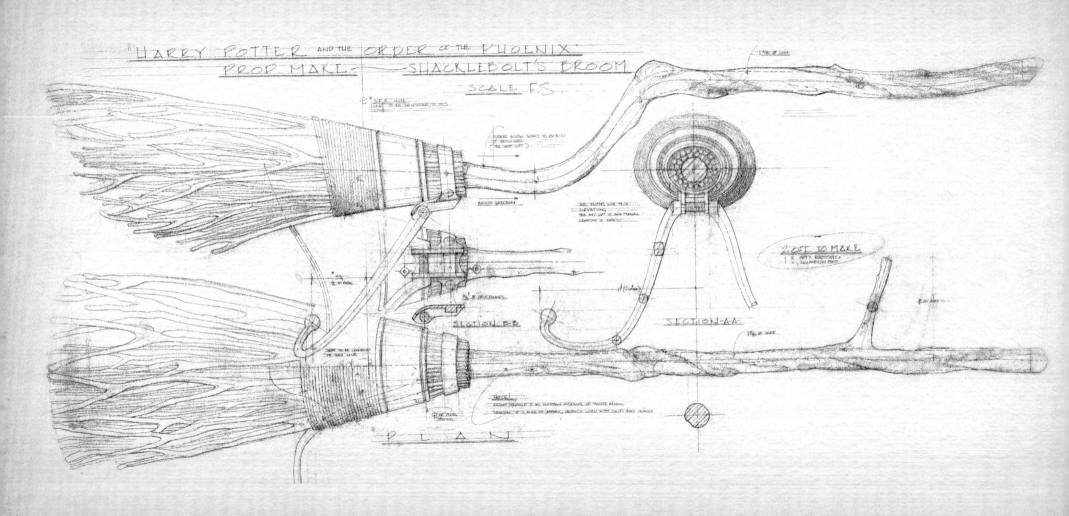

"HARRY POTTER AND THE ORDER OF THE PHOENIX"
PROP MAKE — SHACKLEBOLT'S BROOM
SCALE F.S.

PLAN

SECTION B-B

SECTION A-A

THE BLUEPRINTS

DESIGNING THE FIREBOLT

Concept artist Dermot Power had very specific ideas in mind as he developed the Firebolt broom. For the handle that emerged from the broom's collar, which he called the 'lower crank,' Power wanted an organic twist that elevated into a multi-textured shaft. His original idea to have the collar created from a single band of gold, with the appearance of soft embossing on its underside, changed to two solid silver bands. For the brush section, Power suggested a separate, woven birch 'hood', which would encapsulate the bristle's twigs. Instead of a hood, however, the final version of the Firebolt had two thick birch branches inserted on opposite sides of the lower band that came together in a V over the top of the twigs, giving the impression of a protective hood.

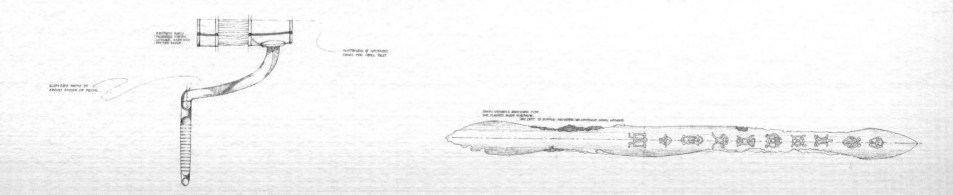

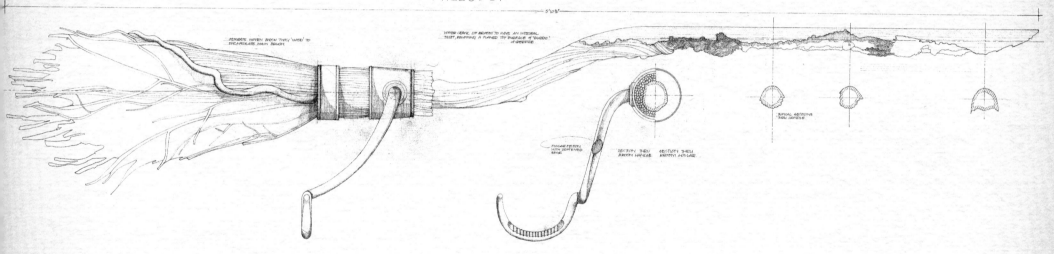

"HARRY POTTER & THE PRISONER OF AZKABAN"
HARRY'S BROOMSTICK "FIREBOLT"   FULL SIZE

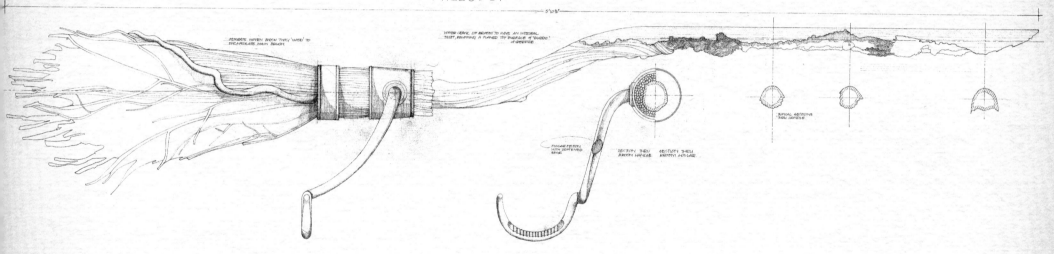

DESIGNING ACTION BROOMS

With several new players on the Gryffindor Quidditch team, now captained by Harry Potter, along with new members on the Slytherin team, the concept artists and draughtspeople drew up ideas for the dozen-plus new brooms needed for *Harry Potter and the Half-Blood Prince*. Three types of 'action' brooms were devised with several interchangeable elements, resulting in the creation of a variety of broomsticks. Metal and leather finishes could be varied, along with shapes of bristle heads and handle angles. The artists also referenced previous brooms and recycled designs – for example, the pedals from Fred and George Weasley's and Tonks's brooms, the handle from Viktor Krum's broom and even hardware from Harry's Firebolt. The draught work, which notes specific handle and bristle-head lengths, is by Amanda Leggatt, Martin Foley and Stephen Swain.

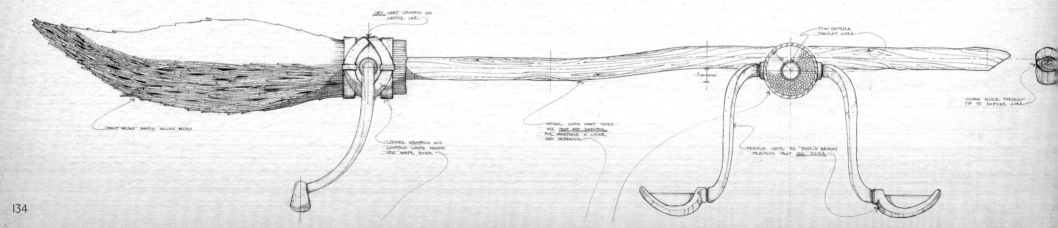

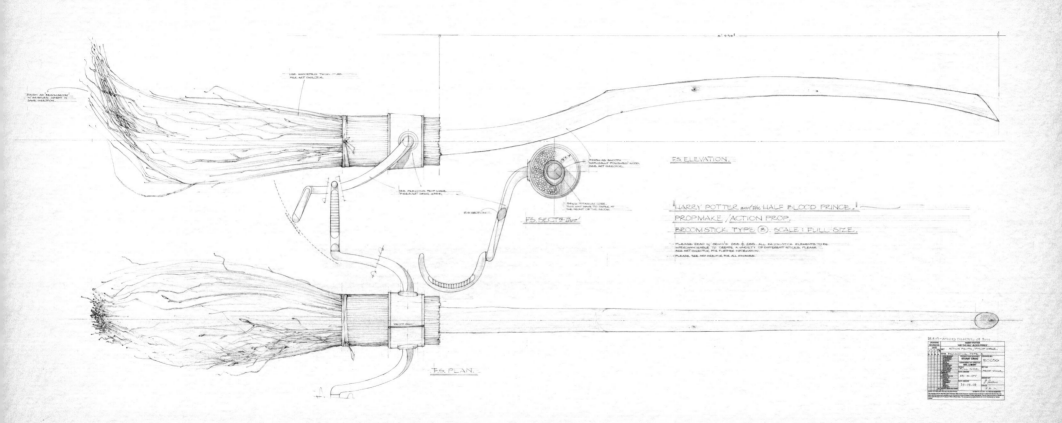

F.S ELEVATION.

HARRY POTTER and the HALF BLOOD PRINCE.

PROPMAKE / ACTION PROP.

BROOM STICK TYPE ③. SCALE : FULL SIZE.

F.S PLAN.

DESIGNING ALASTOR MOODY'S BROOM

Alastor Moody's broom is unique not only in its construction but also in its extensive ornamentation, which draughtsman Gary Jopling suggested for the tip of the handle and bristle-head collar. Another distinctive element that Jopling proposed was an aged metal piece that would cover over the entire shaft. However, for the finished broom, only the top of the handle was given a carved metal jacket, which matched the broom's collar.

Draughtspeople for the Harry Potter films and other movies must have a high level of engineering and architectural skills in order to accurately communicate the detailed information needed before practical construction can start. Due to the intricate structure of Alastor Moody's broom, the draughtspeople who created the blueprint elevations – which give heights, lengths and other dimensions of the piece as well as portraying its finished appearance – had much to consider to ensure that the broom could hold actor Brendan Gleeson properly as it moved on its motion-control rig.

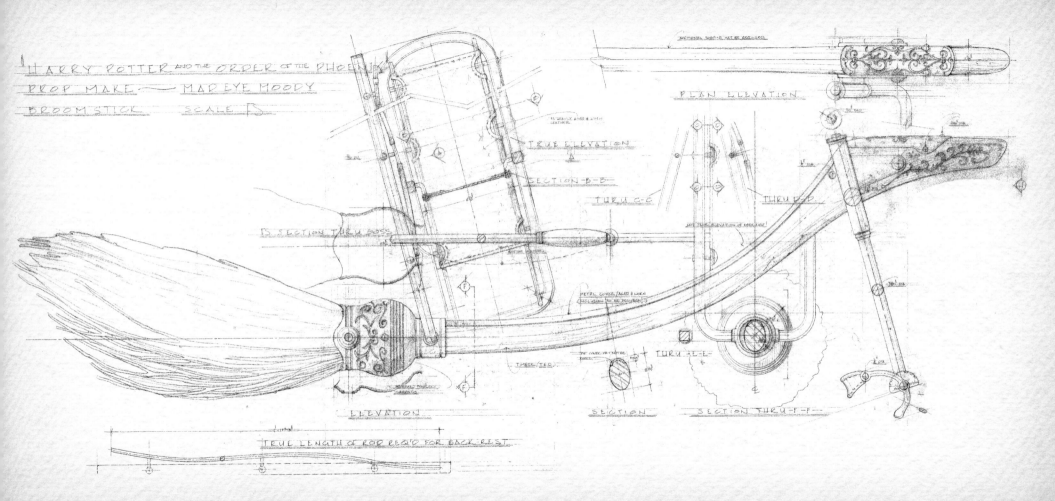

HARRY POTTER AND THE ORDER OF THE PHOENIX
PROP MAKE — MAD EYE MOODY
BROOMSTICK   SCALE B

PLAN ELEVATION

TRUE ELEVATION

SECTION-B-B

THRU C-C   THRU D

IS SECTION THRU BOSS

TURU-E-E

ELEVATION   SECTION   SECTION THRU-F-F

TRUE LENGTH OF ROD REQ'D FOR BACK-REST

DESIGNING ARTHUR WEASLEY'S BROOM

Miraphora Mina really liked her design for Arthur Weasley's broom, but given the opportunity, she would have made changes. "I thought that [as] he loves all things Muggle," she explains, "that he might have turned a double-seat broom into something like those two-person paddle boats. Then, he might have taken bits of other Muggle things and adapted them, perhaps inventing a way to protect his robes from getting caught."

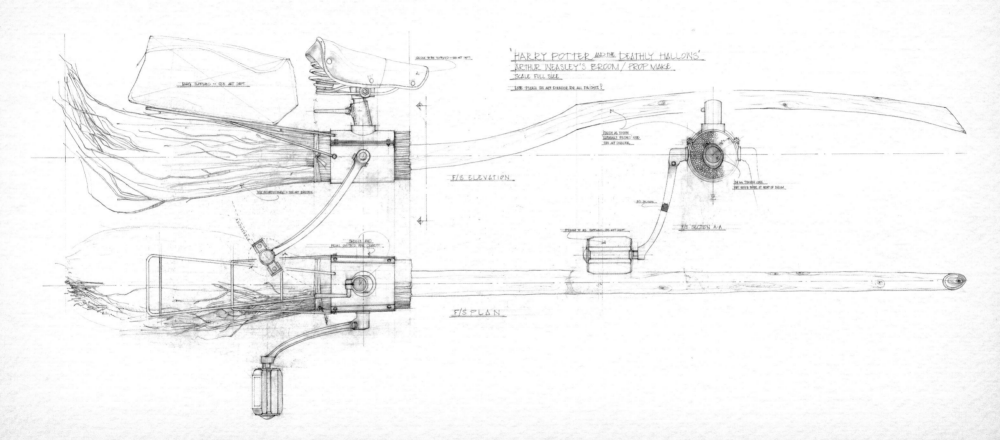

'HARRY POTTER AND THE DEATHLY HALLOWS'
ARTHUR WEASLEY'S BROOM / PROP MAKE
SCALE FULL SIZE

F/S ELEVATION

F/S SECTION A-A

F/S PLAN

DESIGNING RON'S
ROOM OF REQUIREMENT BROOM

The broom Ron Weasley rides while escaping the flames in the Room of Requirement – designed by Julia Dehoff – is the only broom seen in the films with a capped tip, and it has an equally unusual construction to its collar and bristle head. In the final version of the broom, the fender-type apparatus above the bristle head in Dehoff's design was changed from a woven collar to a solid one. This supported the U-shaped stuffed padding, which was reminiscent of American saddles of the 1800s.

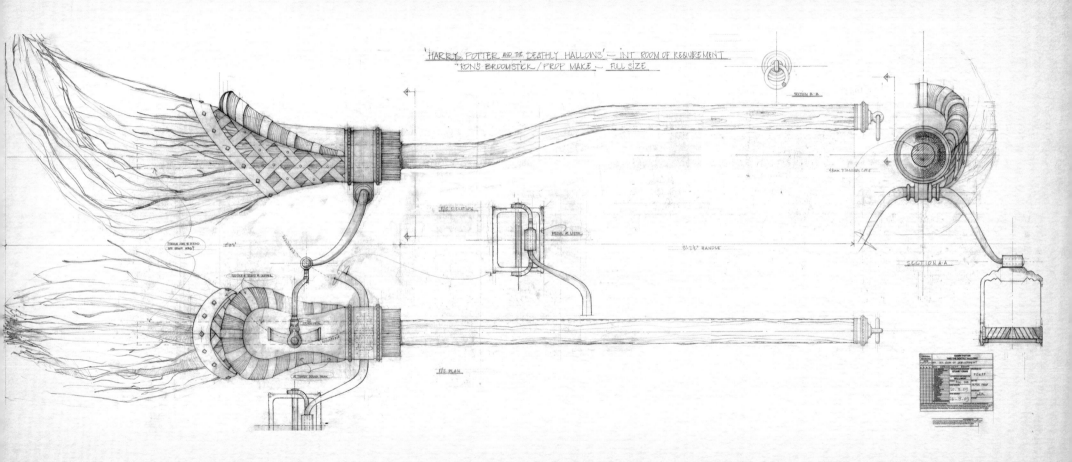

'HARRY POTTER AND THE DEATHLY HALLOWS' — INT ROOM OF REQUIREMENT
"RON'S BROOMSTICK / PROP MAKE — FULL SIZE

SECTION B-B.

F/G ELEVATION

PEDAL IN METAL

3'-3½" HANDLE

SECTION A-A

F/S PLAN

CONCLUSION

One of Daniel Radcliffe's favourite shots in the first Harry Potter movie, *Harry Potter and the Philosopher's Stone*, is the students' first flying lesson, shot on location at Alnwick Castle. "There's something very sweet and innocent about that low-angle shot where the broom flies up into my hand and I sort of smile, pleased with myself," he says. "It's a key moment for Harry." Radcliffe had been looking forward to 'flying' on a broom, though he admits his first experiences were less than thrilling as he dangled in a harness holding a simple, scraggly broom between his legs.

But "the brooms got better over the years," says Greg Powell, stunt coordinator for the Harry Potter films. "They started off with old wrecks and ended with the Rolls Royce of brooms, with seats and handlebars. It wasn't like that at the beginning. They started off as a garden broom and then were modernised, like cars."

The special effects and visual effects teams constantly raised the bar for broom-flying throughout the course of the Harry Potter films. New technologies allowed for broom stunts that were higher, faster and more thrilling. Comfort was improved for the actors, who would straddle a broom in a green-screen room for days on end, surrounded by nearly 360 degrees of wind machines. Quidditch matches became more complicated, but at the same time, more realistic and relatable to audiences who yearned to play along.

"The idea of flying has always been an amazing possibility to me," says actor Alfred Enoch, whose character, Dean Thomas, joins the Gryffindor Quidditch team in *Harry Potter and the Half-Blood Prince*. "Wouldn't having a broomstick, to be absolutely free in the sky, be fantastic?"

BROOM INDEX

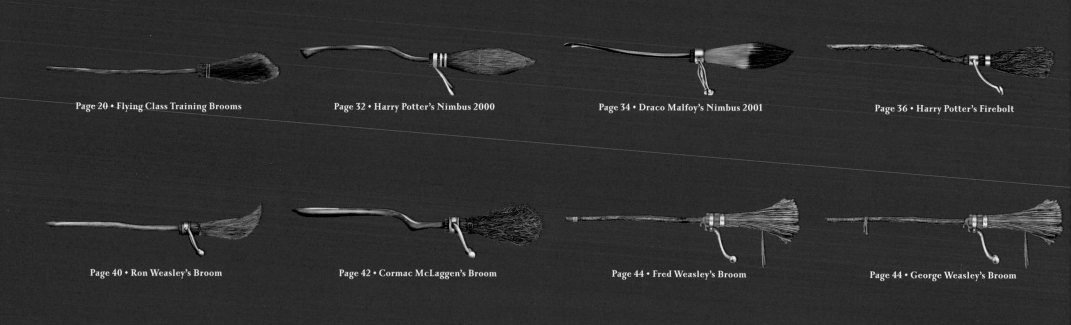

Page 20 • Flying Class Training Brooms

Page 32 • Harry Potter's Nimbus 2000

Page 34 • Draco Malfoy's Nimbus 2001

Page 36 • Harry Potter's Firebolt

Page 40 • Ron Weasley's Broom

Page 42 • Cormac McLaggen's Broom

Page 44 • Fred Weasley's Broom

Page 44 • George Weasley's Broom

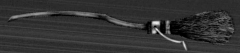

Page 48 • Ginny Weasley's Broom

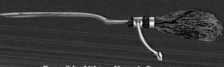

Page 84 • Viktor Krum's Broom

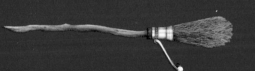

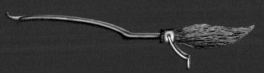

BLOOMSBURY CHILDREN'S BOOKS, Bloomsbury Publishing Plc,
50 Bedford Square, London WC1B 3DP, UK

BLOOMSBURY, BLOOMSBURY CHILDREN'S BOOKS
and the Diana logo are trademarks of Bloomsbury Publishing Plc

First published in the US in 2020
First published in Great Britain in 2020 by
Bloomsbury Publishing Plc

www.bloomsbury.com

A catalogue record for this book is available from the British Library
ISBN: 978-1-5266-2930-2

Publisher: Raoul Goff
Associate Publisher: Vanessa Lopez
Creative Director: Chrissy Kwasnik
VP of Manufacturing: Alix Nicholaeff
Designers: Monique Narboneta & Judy Wiatrek Trum
Senior Editor: Greg Solano
Editorial Assistant: Maya Alpert
Managing Editor: Lauren LePera
Senior Production Editor: Rachel Anderson
Production Director/Subsidiary Rights: Lina s Palma
Senior Production Manager: Greg Steffen
Broom Illustrations by Richard Davies

ROOTS of PEACE ⊕ REPLANTED PAPER

Insight Editions, in association with Roots of Peace, will plant two trees for each tree used in the manufacturing of this book.
Roots of Peace is an internationally renowned humanitarian organisation dedicated to eradicating land mines worldwide
and converting war-torn lands into productive farms and wildlife habitats. Roots of Peace will plant two million fruit and nut
trees in Afghanistan and provide farmers there with the skills and support necessary for sustainable land use.

Manufactured in China by Insight Editions
10 9 8 7 6 5 4 3 2 1